FORT WOOL

FORT WOOL

STAR-SPANGLED BANNER RISING

To Alice Grimes,
Thank you for your help
saving historic Fort Wool!
J. Michael Cobb
2020

J. MICHAEL COBB

With research and photo editors

ED HICKS, WYTHE HOLT AND TIM SMITH

Charleston   London

THE
History
PRESS

Published by The History Press
Charleston, SC 29403
www.historypress.net

First published 2009
Second printing 2012

Manufactured in the United States

ISBN 978.1.59629.574.2

Library of Congress Cataloging-in-Publication Data

Cobb, J. Michael.
Fort Wool : star-spangled banner rising / J. Michael Cobb.
p. cm.
Includes bibliographical references and index.
ISBN 978-1-59629-574-2 (alk. paper)
1. Fort Wool (Va.)--History. 2. Hampton (Va.)--History, Military. I. Title.
F234.H23C59 2009
975.5'412--dc22
2009017632

For my father Mike A. Cobb,
builder during the Great Depression,
during the Second World War,
and in peacetime

CONTENTS

Acknowledgements   9
Introduction   11

Chapter 1   I Shut Myself Up On These Rocks   13
Chapter 2   Siege of the Rip Raps   31
Chapter 3   From Such Nefarious Enemies
                 Good Lord Deliver Us   39
Chapter 4   Scows and Stones   47
Chapter 5   The Wind Whistles Among the Naked Spars   57
Chapter 6   Dose of Heated Granite   71
Chapter 7   Fearful Havoc   81
Chapter 8   Soft Times   99
Chapter 9   The President Is at This Moment at Fort Wool   107
Chapter 10   Great Derricks, Like Deserted Giants   121
Chapter 11   Disappearing Guns   129
Chapter 12   Nothing but Rocks to Throw at the Invader   143
Chapter 13   Deader than Four o'Clock   163

             Notes   171
             Bibliography   183

ACKNOWLEDGEMENTS

Many people have helped to make this project a success. The Earl Gregg Swem Library and the Wolf Law Library at the College of William and Mary in my hometown have been a tremendous resource. The great bulk of the original documents and plans used in this volume was found in the National Archives, both at the main buildings in Washington, D.C., and College Park, Maryland, and at the Branch Depository in Philadelphia, Pennsylvania, where the archivists were extremely helpful and supportive. Other research was accomplished in good style at the Virginia Historical Society and the Library of Virginia, both in Richmond, and at the Norfolk Public Library, where Peggy Hale McPhillips was her usual helpful self, while Robert B. Hitchings was also of great assistance.

Images and other support were generously offered by the Naval Historical Center in Washington, D.C.; the Mariners Museum of Newport News; Terry Hammond at the William E. Rouse Research Library in Hampton; Joe Judge at Nauticus, the Hampton Roads Naval Museum in Norfolk; Cory Thornton at the Portsmouth Naval Shipyard Museum; Gail E. Farr at the National Archives Branch in Philadelphia; Mark Berhow and Bolling Smith of the Coast Defense Study Group; John Weaver, the noted historian of the Third System of coastal defenses; Elizabeth Wilson and Gaynell Drummond at the Hampton Public Library; and Paul Morando and David Johnson at the Casemate Museum of Fort Monroe. In addition, Bolling Smith, Paul Morando, David Johnson, and John Weaver read the entire manuscript and offered many helpful suggestions.

Joe Fudge of the Newport News *Daily Press* generously contributed several images. Elizabeth Panzer made invaluable editorial and research contributions. While Dick Weinert is gone now, he provided much information, companionship, and other kindnesses when he could, and his groundbreaking history of Fort Monroe, *Defender of the Chesapeake*, has proved invaluable.

Acknowledgements

World War II veterans who were stationed at Fort Wool made special contributions of their knowledge, reminiscences, and images. Thanks go to Horace Gifford, Ray Alexander, Walter Scott, and especially Tom Fazenbaker, who was always on call when needed.

A great deal of information and archaeological support was given by Nick Luccketti at the James River Institute for Archaeology in Williamsburg, Virginia, and by David K. Hazzard, archaeologist at the Virginia Department of Historic Resources. All 2009 photographs were taken by Dave on a cold, clear February day, when we renewed our acquaintance with the charms of the Rip Raps, and he generously donated them to the cause.

My colleagues on the staff of the Hampton History Museum have given aid and support over and above the call of duty. All unattributed images come from the Collections of the Hampton History Museum. I wish to recognize the board of the Hampton History Museum Association. Director Jim Wilson of the City of Hampton Parks and Recreation Department continues to give sturdy and welcome support to Fort Wool and to the Hampton History Museum's publication program, of which this book forms a part. His predecessor, Tom Daniels, deserves great praise for having opened Fort Wool to the public. I also extend my gratitude to Director Sallie Grant-Divenuti of Hampton Conventions and Tourism for her prolonged support and efforts in promoting Fort Wool as a tourist destination.

Over many years, the Fort Wool interpreters, known as "Woolies," have shared my passion and taught me much about the Rip Raps. My appreciation also goes to Captain Mike Hebert and the hardy crew of the *Miss Hampton* tour boat, who have brought thousands of visitors to the fort over the years.

The History Press has provided expert guidance through the intricate world of publication and its formatting, which has gone a long way to make this work possible and appealing. I want especially to thank my commissioning editor there, Laura All, for her patience and her expertise in advising the proper preparation of this work at each step of the way, and my manuscript editor, Ryan Finn, for his excellent attention to style and detail.

Tim Smith, historian and seventh-generation York County boat builder, generously donated his time and irreplaceable expertise in photography and preparation of images for this book. He also found several important images that made their way into these pages. Co-workers and friends who have given untold hours to help me in researching, in writing and editing the text, and in finding, arranging, and describing the images—greatly improving the flow and sharpening the detail of this volume—were Ed Hicks and Wythe Holt. We have become known as the Three Musketeers, with apologies to Alexandre Dumas.

INTRODUCTION

After the British navy roamed the American seacoast almost at will during the Revolution and the War of 1812, attacking and sometimes destroying cities, the U.S. government determined that this would never happen again. A system of forts was planned to provide an impervious defense. Two impressive fortifications were planned and built at the entrance to Virginia's fine harbor of Hampton Roads, situated between the mouth of the James River and the southern end of Chesapeake Bay.

North America's largest moated fortification, Fort Monroe, was thrown up on Old Point Comfort, a spit of sandy land on the western side on which Englishmen had placed defensive works for two hundred years. Captain John Smith called it a "little ile fit for a castle." Fort Algernoune had been erected there in 1609 by the Jamestown settlers as a first line of defense against marauding Spanish ships. It was followed by Fort George, a stronger brick and sand rampart, which was destroyed by the great 1749 hurricane. Point Comfort was a natural site for coastal defense works. But what of the other side of the harbor entrance?

The sandy spit there was too distant to sustain a crossfire that would cover the whole channel. The bold answer was to build the eastern-side fort on a man-made island at the edge of the undersea extension of that spit, Willoughby Shoal. Work was begun in 1818 on what would become Fort Wool but was then called Fort Calhoun. This volume tells its story, or perhaps its many stories.

Several presidents of the United States visited the island of stone, beginning with Andrew Jackson, who was so infatuated with the remote site that he made it his summer White House. Abraham Lincoln observed the federal bombardment of Confederate positions preparatory to the Northern capture of Norfolk during the Civil War. Theodore Roosevelt sent his flotilla of great battleships past the island and around the world from Hampton Roads.

A seemingly endless story of Fort Wool concerns the immense difficulties encountered in building the island, then in constructing the fort and, finally, in providing it with appropriate armament. Robert E. Lee supervised its construction for three years, achieving there his first independent command in 1834.

With the turn of the twentieth century, the fort was almost completely modernized, and then again during World War II, as the technology of armament continued to develop, it underwent further modification. The nuclear age has rendered it militarily redundant, and today the island and its huge, often mysterious bits and pieces of fortification are searching for new utility and meaning. It is now a fascinating historical site under the aegis of the City of Hampton, reachable by tour boat.

Chapter 1

I SHUT MYSELF UP
ON THESE ROCKS

President Andrew Jackson sailed on the steamship *Potomac* from Washington down the Potomac River and through the lower Chesapeake Bay in July 1829. His destination was America's best anchorage, Virginia's Hampton Roads, en route to an official inspection of the new dry dock being constructed at Gosport Navy Yard near Portsmouth. He was only three months into his first term, a triumphant beginning marked by a tremulous and uproarious inaugural celebration bibulously attended by his beloved common people. On the voyage, Jackson was escorted by the nation's military leadership: Brigadier General Simon Bernard of the Army Corps of Engineers, Secretary of War John H. Eaton, Secretary of the Navy John Branch, Major General Alexander Macomb, Commodores John Rodgers and Lewis Warrington, and Jackson's personal secretary, army Major Andrew Jackson Donelson. Several of their wives were present also, including Peggy Eaton.

Standing shoulder to shoulder on deck with the president and America's military giants as they approached the entrance to Hampton Roads from its confluence with Chesapeake Bay, Bernard must have been filled with pride as the two huge stone bastions that he had envisioned to guard that entrance emerged into view. From the *Potomac*'s starboard gunwales, Fort Monroe filled the point of land on which it sat. To the leeward stood Fort Calhoun, solitary on an island of rock and a cannon shot across the water. Bernard's waterborne viewpoint was the same that those aboard enemy vessels would have, attempting to breach Hampton Roads. Even though the forts were still undergoing construction, the two battlements loomed, grim and imposing. They would provide a fine defense for the harbor.

At 5:00 p.m. on July 10, the *Potomac* passed in the lee of Fort Calhoun toward its destination, Fort Monroe, where soldiers awaiting their commander-

Hampton Roads, lower right center, has Fort Monroe and the Rip Raps at its eastern mouth. Most places mentioned in this book may be found here. *Casemate Museum, Fort Monroe.*

in-chief stood on the ramparts and near the wharf. Lining the beaches were throngs of civilians, black and white, from the towns near Hampton Roads—Hampton, Norfolk, and Portsmouth—straining for a glimpse of the celebrated man as the vessel docked at the pier. The post's commander, Colonel James House, greeted Jackson warmly. As a military band played the "President's March" and the roar of artillery followed, the president removed his hat with a touch of élan and was escorted to his quarters within the fort amid great ceremony. Entertainment attended by the president flowed into the evening, culminating in a grand fireworks display in the form of wheels and rockets, to the throng's jubilation.

The following day, Saturday, July 11, aboard the steamboat *Hampton*, the presidential party journeyed across the Roads and up the Elizabeth River,

Andrew Jackson, wearing his beaver top hat, which he used to store notes and small items. Engraving, H.B. Hall, 1883, from a painting by Ralph E.W. Earl.

past Norfolk and Portsmouth to the Gosport Navy Yard. As the president sailed by the stately Norfolk Naval Hospital, a battery of twelve-pounders delivered a twenty-four-gun salute. Crucial for Gosport, a decision had been made for the construction of a granite dry dock, only the second in the entire nation. When completed in 1833, it would become a key addition to Gosport's operations. Large enough to handle any ship in the United States Navy, it would generate a great deal of building and repair work for the facility. Commodore James Barron, the navy yard's commandant and a native of Hampton, welcomed the president while workmen at the dry dock assembled to receive him. The yard's gun battery fired a national salute, and honors were paid by the Marine Guard. A local newspaper commented that "the yard[arm]s of the frigate *Constellation* and sloop of war *Erie* were also manned in beautiful style, affording the finest displays we have for a long time witnessed."[1]

On the way back from the dry dock to Fort Monroe, the president decided to make a personal inspection of the progress being made at Fort Calhoun. The *Hampton* was secured to the wharf, and Andrew Jackson first set foot on the granite rocks of the man-made island with an inspiring prospect into the open bay he came to love so well. He was immediately taken with its natural attributes. Without hesitation, according to a local newspaper, he pronounced it "the most efficient of the two" forts. Although at the time it

The *Delaware* entering the huge new dry dock at the Gosport Navy Yard. Andrew Jackson called it a "prodigious floating castle." *Portsmouth Naval Shipyard Museum.*

Early scene of the Rip Raps, with passing watercraft. Buildings have been erected, cranes are in place, and piles of stone ring the island. Engraving; circa 1864. *Harper's Weekly.*

was a good deal less than half finished, he saw that one day it would be a monumental fortification, heavy with guns, standing in the harbor square and ready.[2]

It also had an appeal to him as a location at which he could isolate himself, and he would soon adopt the site as his favorite presidential retreat. Albeit usually for brief intervals, the Hero of New Orleans and the most renowned living American would thereafter return to inhabit this small, relatively empty sphere (Fort Calhoun), transforming it at times into the focal point of American political life, where some of the most consequential Jacksonian decisions about issues confronting the United States were in part forged.

The fort had been named for John C. Calhoun, one of Jackson's rivals for the presidency in 1824 and now his often antagonistic vice president. Calhoun had been serving as secretary of war in James Madison's cabinet when construction had commenced more than a decade earlier.

An irregular surface of granite rigged with cranes and buildings, the isle was starkly silhouetted against the horizon as vessels powered by sail and

A young John C. Calhoun. Portrait, Charles King Bird, circa 1822. *Corcoran Gallery of Art.*

steam swept past. That day it was likely aswarm with weathered laborers shaping the fort's rock walls, which had not yet reached the third level of the anticipated four-tier work. As will be detailed later, the building of the fortification was to pause in 1831 in order to allow the huge pile of rocks forming the island to settle properly.

In 1829, Jackson was troubled. He was devastated by the recent death of his beloved wife, Rachel. She had once been described as the "best story-teller, the best dancer, the sprightliest companion, the most dashing horsewoman in the western country."[3] The widower, aged sixty-one, was frail and in ill health, suffering from head pains and shaking with a consumptive cough. Perhaps, as many thought, he was near death. Jackson also felt overrun and overwhelmed by the multitudes of politicians, constant pressures, and persistent importunities brought to him by his high office and his reputation as the representative of ordinary people.

An ongoing search for solitude and respite brought him to the island's fastness in late August 1829. He surmised that protracted stays would improve his failing constitution and allow him an escape from the capital city's stress. Jackson decided to revisit the island "to spend some days sea bathing." After jostling through a crowd of well-wishers, Jackson departed Washington, once again aboard the *Potomac* and accompanied by Eaton. When he retired for the evening, his thoughts turned to Rachel. Writing to his son Andrew Jr., he inquired about the condition of the grave site at the Hermitage, their home near Nashville: "Whether the weeping willows that we planted around it, are growing, or whether the flowers reared by her industrious, and beloved hands, have been set around the grave as I requested...her memory will remain fresh there as long as life lasts."[4]

Jackson and Eaton were probably not amused at the irony of sojourning at a place honoring their common adversary, the vice president. Allegations of impropriety aimed at Eaton's wife Peggy had become the era's most notorious social contretemps, and Calhoun's wife Floride led the ostracizing of Peggy from polite Washington society. The president was fond of Peggy and carried with him the painful memory of similarly slanderous attacks on his relationship with and marriage to Rachel, and he was outraged. The Peggy Eaton Affair shattered an already tenuous relationship between Jackson and Calhoun.[5] It is probably significant that none of Jackson's surviving letters or papers terms his retreat "Fort Calhoun," always using the name "the Rip Raps" (words which mean chunks of rocks used as a foundation, usually in the water), which was the name given it by locals, adopted by the men building the fort and by those stationed at Fort Monroe. (It was also called "Castle Calhoun" by some of the engineers and general officers.)

Rachel Jackson, the beloved wife of President Jackson. Print, circa 1827. *Library of Congress.*

Cigar box lid featuring Peggy O'Neal Eaton, with Andrew Jackson (left) presenting her flowers and her husband (right) defending her honor in a duel.

After Captain Uriah Jenkins docked the *Potomac*, Jackson and Eaton set up residence at the officers' quarters situated near the foot of the island's principal wharf. The engineer directing the construction was also quartered there, and it was where much of the planning and routine daily business was transacted. Its architecture contained elements of style suggesting the engineers' esprit de corps: the double-story wooden edifice had a veranda with a dual stairway.

The president captured the essence of his new retreat in a letter written the first night he was there. Though he found it "cold, damp, & disagreeable," he was happy. "Tomorrow we commence Bachelors' life, where we will be in perfect retirement, surrounded by a delightful water view, made more pleasant by the constant din of improvement." No din shattered his nighttime peace, however. "Everything is perfectly still & silent as tho we were the only inhabitants of this spot." Jackson was ebullient, filled with optimism about the ability of intelligent, capable humans to order the universe. "The place…shows what system can produce, when the superintendent [Simon Bernard] is acquainted with human nature, and possessing talents to benefit from that knowledge."[6]

Jackson's selection of this secluded seaside setting immediately caused suspicion among his Whig Party rivals and others that the president was gravely ill, far more so than was publicly admitted, and was attempting to conceal his malady from the American people. After all, according to the maleficent story, access to the fort was prohibited with the exception of boats given express authority to dock. The president's many enemies, critical of his July visit to inspect the Gosport dry dock, also charged that he was "moving in the style of Royalty, of getting up a mighty pageant whereby to blind the people, and gull them into an approbation of his principles."[7]

These tales were far from the truth about Jackson and his retreat. He was hiding nothing. And, in contrast to the July visit full of ceremony, he had retired without fanfare "for a few days from the toils of office to a tranquil residence on the Rip Raps." Jackson was there principally for repose but still warmly received citizens, friends, and strangers alike. Norfolk's August 28 *American Beacon* reported that "a single day has, however, not elapsed without frequent visits. No one has ever been denied access to him, and from the warm and friendly manner in which all were received, who presented themselves, it is apparent that seclusion from society was never contemplated." He "is at all times accessible and affordable to those who call on him merely en passant, and appears to enjoy the flow of spirits for an invalid."

The spirits did flow. During this stay, Jackson purchased his and Eaton's provisions from Marshall Parks, proprietor of the Hygeia, a large hotel next to Fort Monroe housing some of the multitude of men gathered to erect Bernard's two fortifications. The assorted sundries that the president acquired offer a glimpse into the "necessities" enjoyed by the presidential party on the island: a gallon of whiskey, ice, candles, coffee, ketchup, English cheese, steaks, and turtle soup. Jackson was ensconced on his island, entertaining and bathing off the wharf.[8]

From the vantage point of the Rip Raps the commander-in-chief could scan the horizon. Directly north across the deep-water channel, Fort Monroe stood on a large, elongated, banjo-shaped sand bar named Old Point Comfort. When completed in 1834, the moat-enclosed fortification would be America's largest and most majestic citadel. Its monumental architecture dominated the roadstead,[9] its grayish and forbidding stone walls, bastions, and water battery seeming to stretch endlessly along the shore. It was designed to mount 380 guns, with the armament fronting Fort Calhoun projecting northeast toward the Chesapeake Bay. Jackson could see another Point Comfort landmark, the Hygeia, adorned with wide verandas and a colonnade, which was rapidly becoming a fashionable watering place. To the right of the Hygeia, the lighthouse built during Thomas Jefferson's administration in 1802 had long been a welcoming sight to weary seafarers.

Star-Spangled Banner Rising

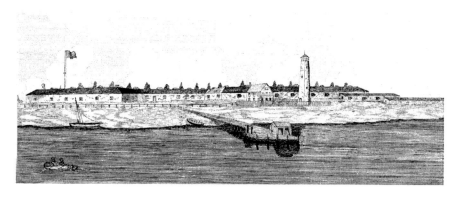

Fort Monroe, featuring the wharf, the Jeffersonian lighthouse, and the keeper's dwelling. Sketch, 1850.

To the east, another narrow, sandy peninsula of land extended from the Norfolk shore. Willoughby Point was sparsely treed and inhabited, and Fort Calhoun had been thrown up on its westernmost underwater extremity, Willoughby Shoal. The waters between the Rip Raps and Willoughby Point were too shallow for ships to pass. To the southeast stretched a wider landmass, Sewell's Point, and beyond it lay the entrance to the Elizabeth River and the ports of Norfolk and Portsmouth. The great harbor of Hampton Roads filled most of the vista afforded to Jackson from the island's dock southward, and on the wooded, lightly settled western shore was Hampton Creek, leading to the town of Hampton. The mighty James River, whose estuary greatly broadened where it joined the Elizabeth and the smaller Nansemond River to become Hampton Roads, was barely visible to the southwest.

General Andrew Jackson had emerged as a national hero after his victory in the Battle of New Orleans during the United States' second war with Great Britain, the War of 1812, named for the year it began. The election of 1828 brought Jackson to the presidency with an unprecedented popular vote. He had run as the candidate of the common man, and his overwhelming success (on his second try) hailed the triumph of popular democracy. Aristocratic critics saw it differently and deemed it "mob rule" as federal offices were redistributed to Jackson's supporters.

Jackson's popularity was legendary. Children were named after him, and people voted for him long after his death. His tenacious character earned him the sobriquet "Old Hickory," while his many foes dubbed him "King Andrew" because of his short temper and high-handedness.

The president had grown to adulthood on the Tennessee frontier in what was then America's wild west. He became a lawyer and eventually rose to be

Wood engraving of a younger Andrew Jackson, by John Vanderlyn, early 1800s. *Library of Congress.*

chief justice of Tennessee, but a rough-and-ready aura always surrounded him. His backcountry origin and innate intellect embodied a notion of popular democracy then emerging throughout the union—that every man has the right and ability to participate in the affairs of government. At the end of an era when most politicians were staunch nationalists—the nullification crisis during Jackson's second term would change all of that—Jackson loved the union fiercely but also supported states' rights and slavery and was a strong advocate for the forced relocation of Native Americans west of the Mississippi River. Jackson's democratic politics transformed society and culture. Great writers of the era such as Nathaniel Hawthorne, Walt Whitman, James Fenimore Cooper, and Washington Irving, as well as historian George D. Bancroft and actor Edwin Forrest, all became Jacksonians. It was a time in antebellum America that would become known as the "Age of Jackson."[10]

By the time he became president, Jackson was aging and weary. The Hero of New Orleans came time and time again to the Rip Raps to escape the capital. On one occasion, he left Washington to avoid the obnoxious fumes of a freshly painted White House. Writing to a friend, he complained about "the repainting of my dwelling, which was I thought, very injurious to my health, and made me very subject to my excruciating head ache." As often is true for people not reared near the ocean, Jackson also found the vast open water vistas of Fort Calhoun startling, captivating, invigorating, and inspiring. His Kentucky friend Francis P. Blair was also struck by the spectacle of the sea in his first days at the Rip Raps: "The first view of the ocean is an era in the life of the backwoodsman—and although I was not...startled...to find the water salt, yet the boundless view, the rolling waves, the canvas which brightens the prospect on all sides, the military strong hold, standing in gloomy strength on the point...have made [a great] impression on my mind."[11]

On the Norfolk or wharf side of the island, the relatively shallow water lapping against the rocks was inviting to Jackson. Salt water and taking in the sea air were widely thought to possess healing qualities. Jackson relished his time on the island "for the benefit of my health, by the sea bathing, and to get free from that continued bustle with which I am always surrounded in Washington, and elsewhere, unless when I shut myself up on these rocks."[12]

The wharf was a convenient platform from which to enter and exit the surf. The sight of the president of the United States partly submerged and enjoying the bathing must have caught the notice of onlookers, though we have no accounts. On one occasion, Old Hickory was stung on the forehead in an encounter with the tentacles of a sea nettle jellyfish, of which many infested the waters, as they still do.[13]

After 1829, at every opportunity Jackson retreated "to this beautiful spot, on the rocks, to enjoy the fine sea breeze and salt water bath." Jackson's time there may have extended his life, and it certainly improved his well-being. The Old Hero's presence, not unexpectedly, attracted national and local attention. As the *Norfolk and Portsmouth Herald* reported: "His hotel at the Rip Raps is a delightful summer residence, freely inviting the breeze over the waters from every point of the compass…The General has found, indeed, a most pleasant and salubrious retreat at the Rip Raps—and as it is the only retreat he has ever made in his life, we hope he will make the most of it."[14]

Jackson did not stay holed up on the island. On Independence Day in 1831—the very day that former president James Monroe died, a fact of course not known yet in Hampton Roads—Jackson went over to Old Point Comfort to preside over an evening of magnificent fireworks. Steamboats conveyed visitors back and forth from Norfolk to the festivities, and an enthusiastic crowd was thrilled by the delightful occasion. This dramatic celebration of independence amplified the importance of Forts Monroe and Calhoun as sturdy defenders of American liberty, as reflected in a passage from a poem of the day: "Here British lions tried their strength before, but would not try again." Occasionally, the general visited acquaintances in the countryside, such as an early August 1835 outing when Jackson climbed aboard the steamboat *Old Dominion* and paid his respects to Richard Drummond, a prominent Norfolk merchant.[15]

Venturing to Fort Calhoun again in the summer of 1833, the president boarded the steamship *Columbia* at Washington. His usual transport, the *Potomac*, which ran regularly between the capital and Norfolk, was unavailable. In order to accommodate the chief executive, the owners of the vessel happily had it deviate from its normal route between Washington and Baltimore in order to deliver him to Hampton Roads. The cruise from Washington to the Rip Raps, a distance of 230 miles, was made in nineteen hours. Much of the trip was on the Chesapeake Bay, known for variable weather and particularly for sudden and vicious storms. George Washington Parke Custis (the grandson of Martha Washington), a fellow passenger on one of these excursions, became apprehensive with the advance of one such rising gale. Jackson, always self-confident, courageous, and reliant on good fortune, said with a smile, "My good friend, you never traveled with me."[16]

While relaxing at his stony Hermitage, Jackson entertained myriad friends, family, and functionaries. In late June 1831, for example, Judge John Overton visited—a Tennessean of great wealth, one of Jackson's stalwart friends and instrumental in shaping his political career. That same summer, Jackson's young secretary, Nicholas P. Trist, found the location "the most delightful spot, as to atmosphere, I have ever been at." Two years later, Jackson received on the island the commanding general of the U.S. Army, Alexander Macomb, who had accompanied him on the fateful dry dock inspection tour in 1829, and Macomb's young aide-de-camp, Major Abraham Van Buren, son of the man who would be Jackson's second-term vice president, Martin Van Buren. Macomb had been awarded a gold medal by Congress for his leadership and heroism at the Battle of Plattsburg, New York, during the War of 1812. When they departed at dawn the next day on board the nation's newest warship *Delaware*, the president watched until they were "just out of sight with a fair wind."[17]

Admirers also sought out the president at his sanctuary. A notable example in late July 1835 was Laban W. Martin, who was granted an interview with the "Distinguished Hero and Statesman" along with his four-year-old son named for Jackson and four neighbors from nearby Nansemond County, Virginia. Martin wrote: "The General arose from his recumbent chair, and with an air of grace and dignity stood to receive me." With his own son, Andrew Jr., and his good friend Blair in attendance, the old man invited everyone to be seated and inquired about their farms. Jackson was moved by being the boy's namesake. Handing young Martin an eagle half dollar, he said, "My son, I present you with the Eagle of your country."[18]

Jackson's family visited from the Hermitage on several occasions. In the summer of 1833, the party included Andrew Jr., the latter's wife, Sarah Yorke Jackson, and several servants. The amiable Sarah became a blessed comfort to the old general in his later years and gave him much happiness by holding the family and household together. Jackson brought the family to the fort for a summer vacation again in 1835.

Accompanying the Jackson entourage was artist Ralph E.W. Earl, often referred to as the "Court Painter" for the many canvasses in which he portrayed the general and his family. Earl had married Rachel's niece, who died soon after the wedding, and he was treated as a family member. The artist was deeply affected by his wife's passing and lost himself in his art, inspired by the island's isolation and panoramic beauty. No doubt the scene became a subject of his artistic imagination.

It was on this occasion that the tidings of the death of General John Coffee reached Jackson. Coffee, referred to by the president as his "favorite friend," had fought side by side with Jackson at Horseshoe Bend during the Creek Indian Wars and at the Battle of New Orleans. Shaken by Coffee's passing, Jackson lamented, "Our philosophy fled and we were unmanned."[19]

Jackson's intimate advisor, Francis Blair, accompanied him to Hampton Roads. Blair summarized the visit: "I spent the month of August and part of September with the President at the Rip Raps—our families occupying the cottages on that pile of rocks." He was touched by Jackson's tenderness to his family, reminiscing:

> *I never witnessed any individual with more tender affection or sympathy than in General Jackson. He had his family at the Rip Raps and his*

An aging Francis Preston Blair. When Andrew Jackson required a publication of his views, he would declare, "Get Blair." Photograph, circa 1870. *Library of Congress.*

courtesy and kindness and love for these strangers to his blood was felt by me as a rebuke to my colder nature and less ardent sympathies with our children. He had his little granddaughter Rachel, a beautiful child about ten months old, named for his wife which he takes to his bosom whenever brought within his reach. I never saw the little bantling in his presence that his eye did not brighten and his affection rise.[20]

Blair was a member of the Kitchen Cabinet, a term used by political opponents of Jackson to describe the collection of trusted friends and unofficial advisors he consulted as president. Joining Blair in the Kitchen Cabinet were Jackson's longtime political allies Martin Van Buren, Amos Kendall, William B. Lewis, and Andrew Donelson, as well as his new attorney general, Roger Brooke Taney.

Jackson brought Blair from Kentucky to Washington to counter Calhoun's supporter Duff Green, editor of the *United States Telegraph*. Blair founded a new paper, the *Washington Globe*, widely read and recognized as the agent of the Jackson regime. In the newspaper, he wrote bombastically, so that persons meeting Blair expected "to find the thunderer of their party, a man of Kentuckian proportions, pistols peeping from his breast-pocket." They were astonished to find him "in person slender and unimposing, in demeanor retiring and quiet, in character amiable, affectionate." Blair had access to the president almost daily and once wrote: "I am never easy till I pay a visit to your office." So it was natural for Blair to be at Jackson's side at the Virginia haven.[21]

Fort Calhoun provided the beleaguered president space and time for solitude, escape, and personal enjoyment. But it also helped to renew Jackson's vigor and strength, and he used the island to debate and hone his responses to major political crises and his positions on major political issues. Chief among these were the Peggy Eaton Affair, the Bank War, and the Nullification Crisis.

Chapter 2

SIEGE OF THE RIP RAPS

While at the Rip Raps, President Jackson carried on a hectic amount of correspondence. He would often use his pen to address the political issues that were roiling not only him but all of American society. The most crucial of these would bring civil war to the United States decades later. Most frequently, he wrote at his desk within the confines of his quarters, perhaps in the evening by candlelight. It was much work, and few copies were made since he did not enjoy the clerical support he had at the White House. In August 1833, he shared his frustration with Roger B. Taney: "My health is improving, but I am much pestered with business, which is sent after me; this will hasten my return to the city, where the burden of so much writing will be lessened."[22]

An important instance involved the infamous issue of Indian removal. John Eaton, taking dictation from Jackson, responded from the island retreat to citizens in New York on September 8, 1829, defending the president's bona fides: "No man in the country entertains towards them better feeling, or has a stronger desire to see them placed in a condition, which may conduce to their advancement and happiness."[23]

The Peggy Eaton Affair seemed to never cease. In late June 1831, the general vented his quarrel against Calhoun, his wife, and the other female gossips of Washington who had maligned Jackson's friend, Peggy Eaton. Jackson railed against his enemies, who "raised the cry w[hore], w[hore] when some of his [Calhoun's] gossips could not today, produce as fair a character as Mrs. Eaton, and against whose chastity more had been said than ever had been against Mrs. Eaton, but Eaton was my friend, it was necessary to drive from me if possible, all who would not bend to Calhoun's ambitious views."[24]

Calhoun's criticism of Jackson's military intervention into Florida in late 1817, combined with an initial denial that he had voiced it, had already made them enemies. An ever-widening chasm between Jackson, much more of a nationalist and the champion of the commoner's voice and right to take part in public life, and Calhoun, an elitist and states' rights advocate, had come to a memorable confrontation at the Jefferson Day Dinner on April 15, 1830. The president, with eyes fixed on his adversary, said, "Our Federal Union—it must be preserved." Calhoun retorted, "The Union—next to our liberty the most dear," adding, "May we all remember that it can only be preserved by respecting the rights of the States and distributing equally the benefit and burden of the Union." This notorious exchange expressed the essence of the sectional antagonisms that would in 1861 bring civil war.[25]

The Rip Raps, a stage of stone on which the drama of the sectional crisis would in part play out, was envisioned by Blair as itself embodying the momentous constitutional contest. For his sympathetic *Globe* readership, Blair crafted a political allegory founded on the exchange, likening the still unfinished and fragmented plight of Fort Calhoun to the chaos that would occur if the union dissolved.

A united and mighty government formed of individual states had mandated and initiated the fort's construction for the protection of the common good, Blair began. Fort Calhoun was thus "*the Castle of the Federal Union*" (Blair's emphasis), and during any assault on it, there must be displayed the "ensign of 'the Federal Union,' [with] the watchword, 'It must be preserved.'" Incomplete, the citadel was yet "a mass of disjointed fragments of stone." Blair inventively asserted that there had been discovered "a yawning fissure in the wall of the southern extremity" of the fort, a thinly disguised reference to Calhoun and the nullifiers. "It will now be taken down and rebuilt under auspices which will secure it against future fissures," Blair concluded, "and when it thus becomes the stay and bulwark of the Union, it will have very properly lost the name of Castle Calhoun."[26]

Also confronting Jackson were the intertwined issues of the Second Bank of the United States—chartered two decades earlier under James Madison—the proper location to invest the funds of the United States if there were no Bank, and the power of wealth. Jackson, the states' righter, did not like national monetary institutions. Jackson, the populist, also expressed his implacable mistrust of the personification of the moneyed society that he hated: bank president and "aristocrat" Nicholas Biddle. The president believed that the concentration of wealth and power exercised by Biddle and his like threatened American democracy and the interests of ordinary people.

On the island, Andrew Jackson had built a modest structure that he utilized as a sanctum to read books, review his correspondence, and tend to issues in a separateness that could not be found in the more accessible officers' quarters. Blair recorded this account: "[T]he old chief had a little hut on the highest point of the rocks looking out to the ocean, where he went to open his mails and talk over matters." The edifice was most likely at the fort's second tier on the island's east end. Its existence would not have impeded the building process because of the suspension of construction in 1831. Jackson's "little pavilion" gave a spectacular view of the Chesapeake Bay, looking toward the open ocean. At his unassuming perch, Jackson, with telescope in hand, scanned the expansive horizon, watching for "distant sail," alone with his thoughts and the sea. Inspired by the view, Jackson took an excursion aboard the U.S. revenue cutter *Jefferson* to visit Capes Henry and Charles.

It was here at the undistinguished hut that the "siege of the Rip Raps," part of the ongoing Bank War, would be waged in the summer of 1832. Nicholas Biddle contrived a "most insidious mode of reaching him in this isolated spot." He organized a campaign for those averse to the contentious withdrawal of deposits from the national bank to flood the secluded president with letters of upset. It was especially infuriating to the general that some of the letters originated from longtime friends. According to Blair:

> *It might almost literally be said to be the point at which Biddle leveled a cannonade from every quarter of the Union...[the] General...like an old eagle, [would] fold his wings for repose on this rock when missiles from every quarter and especially from the cities were poured in upon him in the shape of letters entreating a surrender of the design of removing the deposits.* [27]

Historian George Bancroft recounted that when the bank conflict had reached its greatest height, the president and some friends were standing on the rocks looking out over the water. Would the pressure change his mind and the bank be rechartered? The president remarked: "Providence may change my determination; but man no more can do it than he can remove these Rip Raps, which have resisted the rolling ocean from the beginning of time." [28]

All the while during that summer of 1832, Jackson and Blair were drafting a paper justifying both a veto of the charter and the scheme to transfer the federal deposits to state banks. Kitchen Cabinet members Amos Kendall and Roger B. Taney later contributed to the document. It was a bold assertion

Andrew Jackson, at the time of visiting the Rip Raps. Lithograph, George Endicott, circa 1836. *Library of Congress.*

of Jackson's conception of democracy. The Bank of the United States had evolved, they thought, into a power threatening the continuance of republican government, dangerous to the interests of common folk. Jackson said that most people have

Nicholas Biddle, financier and scholar, edited the Lewis and Clark journals and was Jackson's chief opponent in the Bank War. *Library of Congress.*

Cartoon depicting Biddle as a Satanic figure, with terrified financial "aristocrats," as Jackson destroys the National Bank. Lithograph, Edward Williams Clay. *American Antiquarian Society.*

more to fear from combinations of the wealthy and professional classes—from an aristocracy which thro' the influence of riches and talents, insidiously employed, sometimes succeeds in preventing political institutions, however well adjusted, from securing the freedom of the citizen, and in establishing the most odious and impressive Government under the forms of a free institution.

The renewal of the bank charter from the United States, contrary to the will of the people, would weaken the office of the president and the federal government as a whole and would be "inconsistent with the happiness and liberties of the people."[29]

Soon the president followed through on his promise to veto the bank's recharter. Then the government placed all of its deposits into what Jackson's enemies called his pet banks—politically selected state banks. Writing to Vice President Van Buren from his hut on the rocks in late July 1833, Jackson stated: "I am busy, all my working hours, reviewing the Bank question, and the propriety of removing the deposits to the incorporated banks of the states…a strong case can be made out."[30]

The Nullification Crisis brought into the open the long-standing antipathy existing between Jackson and Calhoun. South Carolinian John C. Calhoun championed the doctrine of nullification, which elevated states' rights above the union by claiming to render invalid any exercise of federal authority within the boundary of a state whose legislature chose to assert its superiority. In 1832, South Carolina declared the federal Tariff Act void within its borders, and this produced a national furor. Corresponding with a fellow officer in December of that year, Second Lieutenant Robert E. Lee, an army engineer overseeing the construction of Fort Calhoun, exclaimed: "There is nothing new here or in these parts, [except] Nullification! Nullification!! Nullification!!!"[31]

In an angry letter drafted on the Rip Raps, the president denied the legality of that "absurd and wicked doctrine." He successfully urged Congress to pass a Force Bill, specifically empowering him to enforce the tariff in South Carolina, with troops if necessary. Jackson wrote from the island in early August 1833:

> *In the end* [nullification,] *if not frowned down by every lover of liberty and a government of laws,* [will] *destroy our happy form of government that secures to all prosperity and happiness; whilst nullification leads to disunion, wretchedness and civil war.*

Jackson soon proposed a more moderate tariff act, which Congress accepted, ending the crisis as South Carolina rescinded its nullification order.[32]

South Carolina's defiance of federal authority once again reached the president while he was at the fort. In early August 1835 (fully twenty-five years before the Civil War), a Charleston mob ransacked a federal post office and destroyed "incendiary" abolitionist tracts. Jackson steadily and publicly maintained that these publications should have been delivered according to law, that is, only to those who had subscribed and not freely distributed. However, Jackson, a member of the slaveholding class, writing to Postmaster General Amos Kendall, expressed his private scorn for those who sent the tracts: "I have read with sorrow and regret that such men live in our happy country. I might have said monsters—as to be guilty of the attempt to stir up amongst the South the horrors of servile war."[33]

The newspapers, covering in great detail the political issues of the moment and the actions and speeches of political figures, made the Rip Raps well known; ordinarily, however, not much was offered about Fort Calhoun except that it was under construction and located on a pile of rocks in Hampton Roads. Jackson's association with the Rip Raps made it a recognizable place to a large number of Americans. Many people visualized the Hermitage, the White House, and the Rip Raps as the places where the president resided. Additionally, they were aware that important decisions affecting their financial and political well-being were made there.

Being cloistered in this favored spot probably brought the president clarity of mind and the energy to marshal his thoughts and craft reasoned responses to various economic, social, and political challenges confronting the country. The Richmond *Enquirer* was of the opinion that life at the Rip Raps would "restore several years of life and health to the President."[34]

Chapter 3

FROM SUCH NEFARIOUS ENEMIES GOOD LORD DELIVER US

Many Americans in the Jacksonian era feared the British. When Andrew Jackson was a youth in South Carolina, near the end of the Revolution, he had refused to shine the boots of an arrogant British officer, and for the rest of his life he retained a deep crease in his skull from the resulting sword blow, which he sometimes angrily demonstrated to onlookers. The British ruled the seas and had fired on many American coastal towns during the Revolution, causing dangerous conflagrations and much damage. This, of course, included towns throughout the southern Chesapeake region such as Norfolk and Hampton.

Two systems of coastal fortifications resulted from these depredations. The first, hastily thrown up around towns and near important rivers and harbors during the approximate period of 1794–1807, and the second, built in the approximate period of 1807–1812, were earthworks revetted with masonry and/or timber. Several forts resulted. Important among these were Fort Norfolk, Fort McHenry in Baltimore Harbor, and Fort Mifflin near Philadelphia. During peacetime, however, many of these works languished and deteriorated for want of government funding.

When hostilities commenced again with the British in the War of 1812, these fortifications proved insufficient because not enough had been built. In addition, although often valiant, the American army and navy failed to defend the nation. Culminating a devastating series of defeats on land and sea, the British army routed the Americans at Bladensburg, Maryland—with President Madison and some of his cabinet as horrified onlookers—and marched unhindered into Washington, burning the capitol, the White House and other public buildings.

In Hampton Roads, British rear admiral Sir George Cockburn's vessels attacked Norfolk and burned and plundered the town of Hampton in

Rear Admiral Sir George Cockburn, with Washington in flames. Portrait, John James Hall, 1817. *Library of Congress.*

British troops, having fired the capitol, retreating after sudden rainstorm that saved many other Washington buildings. Wood engraving, 1876. *Library of Congress.*

1813. A Virginia woman, upon hearing the news from Hampton, wrote that the enemy

> *exhibited deeds of infamy and barbarity* [of] *which none but British savages could have been so callous and lost to the tender feeling of human nature. They pillaged the place of every article they could convey...they murdered the sick and dying and committed the most hard and cruel insults to the defenseless young ladies. From such nefarious enemies good Lord deliver us, is the prayer of your affectionate sister.*[35]

Jackson's victory at New Orleans was one of the few successes that American arms achieved, and he employed news about the British outrage at Hampton to instill determination in the citizens to resist the invader. Another success was achieved at Fort McHenry, whose excellent defensive position managed to keep the marauding British from sacking Baltimore. This is why Francis Scott Key's famous poem about the battle, later made into the national anthem, says that, the next morning, "the flag was still there."

With the ratification of the Treaty of Ghent and the cessation of hostilities in 1815, James Madison and his secretary of state, James Monroe,

The British fired about 1,700 shells during the Fort McHenry bombardment. A British landing party was repulsed with great loss. Print, J. Bower, 1816. *Library of Congress.*

determined to keep such disasters from happening again by greatly bolstering the nation's defenses.

In particular, the president was sensitive to an enemy using the water route for invasion. Madison believed that with "an enemy powerful in its marine, as evinced during the late, as well as during the Revolutionary War," it would be necessary to augment the defense of the lower Chesapeake. In the spring of 1816, that defense consisted merely of ships—two armed schooners, two gunboats, and eight or ten barges. It was hoped that several steam frigates would be added. For another part of the defenses, Madison proposed to follow the lesson of Baltimore's harbor and "fortify strongly Old Point Comfort, so as to afford protection to vessels coming in and going out of the bay."

Madison appointed a mixed commission of naval officers and army engineers, including Commodores John Rodgers and Stephen Decatur and Captain David Porter, to explore the merits of fixed defenses on Chesapeake Bay and Hampton Roads. They considered a variety of approaches and plans. Lieutenant Colonel George Bomford of the army engineers believed that

> *a regular fortification on Old Point Comfort, and a castle on the nearest part of Willoughby's shoal (called the Rip Rap), [a] distance [of] eighteen hundred yards, might, with the aid of a well organized flotilla, not only*

Henry Clay. Photograph of print, circa 1861, probably made much earlier. *Library of Congress.*

cover the James and Elizabeth Rivers from the attempt of a superior naval enemy, but the latter would threaten the rear of any armament that would pass up the bay.[36]

War Hawks Henry Clay, Speaker of the House, and Senator John C. Calhoun—who had advocated entry into the recent conflict with Great Britain—led the way. On January 16, 1816, Clay advocated a federally funded internal improvement program to "bind and connect us together," creating fortifications as well as canals, roads, and turnpikes. Speaking on the floor of the House, he insisted that

> *national independence was only to be maintained by national resistance against foreign encroachments; by cherishing the interest of the people, and giving the whole physical power of the country an interest in the preservation of the nation...construct military roads and canals that the facilities of transportation may exist of the men and means of the country to points where they may be wanted...I would provide steambatteries* [gunboat barges] *for the Mississippi, and for the Chesapeake...In short...I would act, seriously, effectively act, on the principle that in peace we ought to prepare for war.*[37]

America's stalwart French ally during the Revolution, the Marquis de Lafayette, recommended Simon Bernard to Madison for the huge task of supervising the design of the new fortifications. Bernard was a renowned French military engineer who had campaigned with Napoleon Bonaparte. Madison accepted and Congress agreed. In the winter of 1816, Secretary of State James Monroe, a former minister to France and recently acting secretary of war, wrote to inform Andrew Jackson of the Frenchmen's appointment since Jackson was one of the country's foremost military figures. Monroe assured Jackson that Bernard was a "modest, unassuming man, inferior to none in reputation and talents; if not first." Jackson came to admire Bernard's work.[38]

Congress mandated that a board, consisting of Bernard as chair, three senior army engineers, and one naval officer, plan a system of fortifications to defend the coast. The Bernard Board recommended that fifty-three forts be sited in harbors along the Atlantic and along river ways from Maine to the Gulf Coast. Many of the installations were to be erected on natural or man-made islands. Although only forty-two were actually completed, this project would become the republic's most costly and extensive building program up to that time.

The defense of Hampton Roads was imperative and became the board's first priority, along with the defenses of Mobile Bay and New Orleans. The Bernard Board followed its predecessor in envisioning companion forts, one positioned on Old Point Comfort and the other located on an engineered island less than a mile away, occupying "the Rip Rap shoal with a castellated fort; the channel between that shoal and old Point Comfort with a boom raft; and Old Point itself with an enclosed work." The strongholds would protect the roadstead entrance and secure it for the United States, safeguarding the interior waterways emptying into the Roads.[39] The design of the forts has

Simon Bernard, wearing French army uniform. Edouard Baille, 1863. *Casemate Museum, Fort Monroe.*

always been attributed to Bernard, and he took the lead, but the final result was a collaboration among the board members.

Although John C. Calhoun understood that the installations were defensive only—"like a shield without a sword" if the navy were not there too—he still approved their construction. As he said in a letter to Virginia's governor,

> [W]hen we consider the importance of Old Point Comfort, situated at the entrance to an immense bay, and at the mouth of the spacious and commanding harbour of Hampton Roads, an expenditure to erect strong works upon it, which will protect all that part of Virginia watered by the James River and render safe the Town of Norfolk and the Navy yard at Gosport, will appear...justifiable.

In addition, the government proposed to establish one of the nation's largest naval depots along the James River at Burwell's Bay, which would demand such protection.[40]

The Chesapeake Bay and its vital coastal trade would now have protection. Any shipboard foe would be placed at a strategic disadvantage, being compelled to anchor in Lynnhaven Inlet near Cape Henry and march overland in order to threaten regional towns. The names given these new forts, Monroe on Old Point and Calhoun on the island, demonstrated their great importance by honoring the sitting president and secretary of war.

The fortified isle would bear the name of one of America's foremost statesmen in peace and in war. In 1807, Calhoun first became prominent in the United States when as a nationalist and fledgling war hawk he demanded that the nation declare war against Great Britain after a naval encounter off Cape Henry during which the British vessel *Leopard* boldly snatched sailors from the smaller American frigate *Chesapeake* to serve in the Royal Navy. Eventually, this and other disputes led to the War of 1812, during which Calhoun, now a senator, did everything in his power to defeat the invader. For the next two decades, the oratory and statesmanship exhibited by Calhoun and his colleagues Henry Clay of Kentucky and Daniel Webster of Massachusetts would shape every great issue of the day.

James Monroe had been a soldier during the Revolution, and as president he advocated a strong national defense policy. In the spring and summer of 1819, Monroe and Calhoun reconnoitered the emerging new system of fortifications, including those being erected at Hampton Roads. With regard to Fort Calhoun, they saw only an expanse of water, a scow or two containing loads of rocks, and a mass of building materials on Old Point Comfort. The creation of the island would be a gigantic undertaking.[41]

Chapter 4

SCOWS AND STONES

Construction at Castle Calhoun commenced at the time of a major economic depression that ensued following the Panic of 1819. Myriad smaller state banks and a number of small businesses were ruined. A great number of people were out of work and were forced to do without. Congress had also severely reduced appropriations for defense. Thus, there was little other work obtainable in the area, public or private.

The building of Forts Calhoun and Monroe offered a respite in the crisis to some. These were vast projects needing numerous men and would require many years to complete. Hundreds of men, skilled and unskilled, traveled to Old Point Comfort in hopes of finding work on the two new fortifications.

Likewise, local business was stimulated by the work on the Hampton Roads ramparts. This workforce had to be housed and fed. The War Department's contracts were chiefly with Virginia and Maryland firms, for an immense quantity of building materials including stone, brick, sand, timber, and iron, all of which had to be provided and transported.

War Secretary Calhoun requested Virginia governor Thomas Mann Randolph to consent to the cession of jurisdiction over Old Point Comfort and the Rip Raps, and the War Department endeavored to acquire the land, but it encountered opposition from Virginia state authorities. At first, worried that the forts could be nullified by a hostile naval blockade and upset that invaders might still come ashore at Lynnhaven, Virginians demurred and postponed the cession. Governor Randolph said that "a majority in Virginia would have preferred that the U.S. should have given the money to the Navy, which they are about to expend at Old Point" for the two forts. Ships would be offensive as well as defensive. But eventually, in March 1821, after much delay and with construction of both forts actually two years underway, the Virginia General Assembly gave in and conveyed by deed to the federal government several hundred acres on Old Point Comfort and fifteen acres of submerged ground on the edge of Willoughby Shoal. There was a provision in the deeds that if the United States were to abandon or use the property for any purpose other than national defense, the land would revert to the Commonwealth of Virginia.[42]

Work began unhurriedly. On November 30, 1819, Lieutenant Colonel Charles Gratiot, the engineer directing the project, reported to the army's chief engineer, Lieutenant Colonel Walker K. Armistead, that no substantial progress on the defenses had been achieved. He explained that the requirement of copying the plans in Washington for Forts Monroe and Calhoun could not be completed until late into the building season, which had created delays in the construction process. The slow task of gathering both building materials and a considerable workforce for the next summer's building season thus had time to be accomplished. Gratiot assured his superior that the impending project would be "push[ed] with vigor."[43]

At Old Point Comfort, under the direction of contractor Bolitha Laws, the preparations included erecting several sturdy wharves utilized for unloading stone, sand, and other construction materials. Temporary structures were built for worker housing, storehouses, and workshops, a well was excavated, and contracts were let to Hampton boat builders for two scows and a barge. More than one million bricks were made on site at Mill Creek. About 20 stonemasons were hired—"only good workers" were needed—at $1.75 per day. Roughly 150 "hale and hearty" laborers—"blacks would be preferred"—were assembled at $0.40 per day plus meals. Ox and horse carts, teams, and drivers were taken on to move the many tons of materials.[44]

Across the channel, the isle, composed of riprap, was to be carefully shaped. The chief of engineers in late summer 1818 directed "the planting of a number of anchors and the mooring of buoys to be used by vessels discharging stone." A lower layer of smaller rocks (comprising four-fifths of the whole island) would be covered with a stratum of larger blocks weighing up to one thousand pounds each to "resist the violence of the sea." Savvy stone contractors advised the War Department to intermingle smaller stones with the top layer of more massive blocks in order to prevent shifting.[45]

Quarries scattered along the Chesapeake Bay watershed would yield most of the granite for the island, walls, and load-bearing piers of both forts. The material was largely extracted by quarrymen at Havre de Grace and Port Deposit, Maryland, near the confluence of the Susquehanna River with the Chesapeake Bay, and from quarries near the Great Falls of the Potomac River. To a lesser extent, stone was obtained from the falls of the James River and from quarries near Petersburg. Some granite was brought from as

Charles Gratiot. Portrait, Thomas Sully, 1830. *West Point Museum of Art Collection, U.S. Army Military Academy.*

far away as New York. Stone from the nearby York River failed to meet the necessary specifications for use.

Port Deposit granite, light bluish-gray in color, was highly prized and was also used in the construction of Fort Delaware near Philadelphia, Forts McHenry and Carroll in Baltimore, the United States Naval Academy in Annapolis, and the Treasury Building in Washington.[46]

Chesapeake Bay scow schooners and sloops, all under sail, were utilized to transport granite to Hampton Roads. These work boats were fashioned to carry heavy burdens in shallow water. Built by the men who sailed them, each vessel was distinctive. The flat-bottomed schooners—rigged with fore and aft sails, featuring straight sides and square ends to allow more room for cargo, and using centerboards and leeboards rather than deep keels—weighed about ninety tons. The smaller scow sloops were similar in design but rigged differently.[47]

The names of many of the scows that conveyed the stones to the Roads saluted rising national allegiance and exuberant national pride. The men who worked the water were jaunty and independent souls. Naturally, most of their vessels were christened after people familiar in their lives or were named from the owner's imagination. Typical were *Catherine Ann*, *Elizabeth*, *Rebecca*, *High Flyer*, and *Good Return*. Scores of the sailors had fought in the recent conflicts with Great Britain, and they blazoned in rough fashion their nationalist sensibilities on their vessels' sterns. From the Revolution came such names as the *General Washington*, the *Lafayette*, and the *General Putnam*. The *General Jackson*, the *Commodore Peary*, and the *Henry Clay* were proud declamations of patriotism from men who had championed the country during the War of 1812. Further, several names signified that Jackson's common man increasingly perceived himself to be a full American, having a voice in politics and the nation's affairs: the *Independence*, the *United States*, the *Patriot*, the *Resolution*, the *True American*, and even the *Whig*, perhaps from a Jacksonian opponent. Old identifications lingered, as suggested by the *Britannia*.[48]

An inspector and his assistant had the responsibility of receiving and examining the stone blocks as they arrived aboard the ragtag scows, appraising the material to ensure that it met the War Department's specifications as to size, weight, quality, and quantity.[49] Meticulous accounting was imperative because of a lingering controversy over possible corruption in the acquisition of the stone.

Congressional investigations into the stone contracts for Fort Calhoun occurred in 1822 and 1826–27. Frustration, confusion, and claims of impropriety surrounded their awarding and became a national issue. The "stone affair" reflected adversely on the reputation of Secretary Calhoun and the War Department and was the genesis of a shadow that would forever plague the Rip Raps citadel.

The controversy stemmed from an agreement in 1818 under which Elijah Mix was to supply stone for the Rip Raps. Mix was a brother-in-law of Christopher Van Deventer, chief clerk of the War Department and a strong supporter of Calhoun, then secretary of war. In 1822, Congress found that Van Deventer had acquired from Mix a half interest in the contract shortly after its execution. Testimony further revealed that Calhoun had advised Van Deventer that, although there was no legal impediment to the United States employee's investment, such involvement might be open to question by critics. Van Deventer denied that he had exerted any influence in the awarding of the contract.

Fresh allegations that Calhoun was financially interested in the contract appeared in the Alexandria, Virginia *Phoenix Gazette* on December 28, 1826. In 1818, Mix had written a letter to Satterlee Clark—a political opponent of Calhoun, who had dismissed him from his position as paymaster in the War Department for failing to settle his accounts—stating that Calhoun had also been given a share of the profits. Clark did not make the letter public until late 1826, which then provided the basis for the allegation in the *Phoenix Gazette*. The next day, Calhoun, now vice president,[50] requested that the House of Representatives investigate the charges. The House appointed a select committee to conduct its inquiry, and on February 13, 1827, it reported that Calhoun was not financially involved, rejecting Mix's entire testimony on the grounds that he was not a reliable witness.[51]

The Mix contract affair inflicted irreversible damage to Calhoun's reputation. Writing to Andrew Jackson before they became enemies, Calhoun charged that his political adversaries had orchestrated the affair and protested that "a man guilty of forgery, swindling and perjury, was artfully got up to blast my private reputation" and also referred to Mix as a "perjured wretch."[52]

Amid these political clashes, the delivery of the stone continued. Working on the open water was dangerous. Maneuvering a vessel to the proper spot was difficult, and the act of offloading the stone was perilous. The maneuver could be accomplished only by securing each end of the boat to one of the anchors placed there in 1818 and unloading the stone directly over the side. The large, jagged rocks often damaged the aged wooden hulls and gunwales of the watercraft. As the island grew taller and rocks were nearer the surface, the boats were "subject to constant irritation and thumping against the sharp edges of the rocks…occasioned by the swell and agitation of the sea and exposed to increased wear and injury." Proprietors also found it difficult to secure enough vessels to haul the material.[53]

The threat of drowning loomed. Boats unloading materials and provisions could be pounded by winds and seas. The scows were not seaworthy in turbulent water, often finding it difficult or impossible to make the channel crossing. A particularly heavy storm in 1834 caused several vessels bringing stone to the site to run aground on the nearby Hampton Bar. One of them split open, from which "a child, two women and a man with a broken thigh were rescued while [it] was sinking."[54]

Alexander Macomb. Portrait, Thomas Sully, 1829. *West Point Museum of Art Collection, U.S. Military Academy.*

Weather and the ever-changing sea often dictated the labor cycle and the working conditions. Occasionally, the water surface was as smooth as glass, or swells rolled slow and easy. Often, however, the water became choppy, gigantic waves crowned with whitecaps tossed boats and scowmen around, and sometimes terrible hurricanes and northeasters battered the worksite.

The Marquis de Lafayette. His skillful actions at Yorktown contributed to Cornwallis's surrender. Portrait, Joseph Desire Court, 1792. *Chateau de Versailles*.

This photograph shows something of the island that Lafayette saw, rough courses of well-fitted granite breaching the waves. The high tide mark is evident. Photograph, 2009. *David K. Hazzard.*

The Rip Raps was designed to withstand the worst damage that wind and water could inflict.

In late November 1821, the pile of stone had not yet broken the surface. Alexander Macomb reported to Calhoun that it contained 102,000 perches of stones. Construction was progressing normally with the exception of that September's hurricane and the resulting heavy surf, which had dislodged a few of the rocks near water level.[55]

Three years later, much had changed. The island was now visible above the waves, some buildings had been built, and construction apparatus was everywhere. The Marquis de Lafayette, the celebrated Frenchman who fought valiantly to secure independence during the Revolution, visited Fort Monroe in the course of his 1824 Grand Tour of America to marvel at the fortification that formed the American *chef-d'oeuvre* of his countryman Simon Bernard. From Old Point Comfort, Lafayette made the channel crossing to the Rip Raps and strode on the open rocks. While there was not much of Bernard's design to see yet, the island itself was impressive, and with a look at the plans and an exercise of his imagination the aging general could grasp the impressive fortification that Bernard and his board had visualized.[56]

Lafayette continued to be shocked by the existence of enslavement in America, believing the institution inconsistent with the republican values that had brought him across the Atlantic to risk his life in bloody revolution. Surely the presence of black men forced to toil on the defenses intended to secure the country's freedom only made the inconsistency more glaring.[57]

Notable headway had been achieved on the Virginia bastions, and Charles Gratiot was undeniably well pleased. At Old Point Comfort, Fort Monroe was beginning to present a "formidable appearance." Thus far, Fort Calhoun's understructure seemed to be solid, withstanding the "violence of the sea." Gratiot reported that the Rip Raps "already exhibits to the eye the advantage which this position, in connection with Fortress Monroe possesses in defending Hampton Roads."[58] Eventually, the scows would deposit sufficient material to form a plane of rocks rising to seven feet above mean low water, on which Bernard's magnificent fortification could be erected.

Chapter 5

THE WIND WHISTLES
AMONG THE NAKED SPARS

Fort Calhoun was dedicated with a flourish in the fall of 1826. It coincided with the jubilant national celebration of the fiftieth anniversary of the Declaration of Independence, and Americans were feeling high-spirited and triumphant. After two struggles with Great Britain, everyone knew now that liberty would not only endure, it would also expand westward across the continent. Thomas Jefferson's Louisiana Purchase was drawing thousands to the interior. Americans possessed an overwhelming assurance that divine providence guided and protected a people destined to advance their culture and ideology. When Jefferson and John Adams both died on July 4, 1826, huge numbers imagined that the Almighty had underscored the nation's importance, in a sense validating the American dream of freedom.

On September 17, the first stone at Fort Calhoun was set, dedicating this "great work of national defense." The event was a soldierly remembrance of American valor during the recent war. No doubt to some extent the day's rhetoric compensated for the stinging military defeats inflicted by the hated invaders a decade previously. Hezekiah Niles's Baltimore paper, the *Niles Register*, the country's most popular newsweekly, gave exuberant coverage to the affair.

The scene on the island's rocky plane was impressive, as numbers of Andrew Jackson's comrades in arms from the War of 1812 gathered. Jacob Brown, the commanding general of the army, would perform the honor of positioning the structure's first granite block. Colonel Abraham Eustis, the commander of Forts Calhoun and Monroe, and Colonel Gratiot also graced the occasion. A contingent from the Fort Monroe garrison assembled among the island's few buildings. The ceremony commenced with a prayer and music by the Artillery School of Practice band, which drifted across the open water.

Major General Jacob Brown. Engraving from portrait in 1814 series of American heroes. *Library of Congress.*

Star-Spangled Banner Rising

Brown's remarks recognized the crucial importance of the 1812 hostilities to the fort's origins:

> *In thus assisting my brother officers in laying a corner stone of this great work, in honor of the seventeenth of September 1814* [when Brown's forces had distinguished themselves in fighting on the Niagara frontier in New York], *I must be permitted, in gratitude to our Common Parent, piously to remember those exalted spirits, who...during the Siege of Erie, endeavored to sustain the moral power of their country.*

A master mason put the stone in place for Brown's symbolic hammer stroke, and the color guard bent to its task. During a cannon salute, the nation's flag was hoisted for the first time over the beginnings of Fort Calhoun, as "the Star Spangled Banner rising in majestic grandeur, through the dense canopy of smoke that o'er hung the island, proclaimed to the world the birthday of another bulwark of liberty."[59]

The Fort Calhoun project was extravagant, ultimately costing more than Fort Monroe. By October 1, 1825, the government had committed $605,767.25 to the endeavor. More than 152,965 perches of stone had been delivered for $470,278.70. Bricks numbering 2,592,916 for the casemate arches were acquired for $19,827.82. More than 315,800 iron rods had cost $3,268.49, and "contingencies" totaled $112,594.29.

While at this time the United States Army was small, it was thought essential to garrison 200 regular troops at Fort Calhoun. In times of peril, it was believed that 1,130 men would be called for. All had to be protected. Thus, it was important to house the troops in large barracks embedded in the fort's wall on the south or "gorge" side, relatively far away from the areas that were imagined to be possibly under attack. This would also leave the parade ground clear. Unfortunately, these troop quarters were never constructed.

Fort Calhoun, if completed according to its original design, would have been a monumental work, a tribute to Bernard and his board. The island was shaped like a boomerang or an inverted wing, the area of its plane totaling about five acres. The walls would consist of four levels, three tiers of casemates and a barbette. Exactly 232 pieces of artillery were to be mounted in the casemates and looming on the barbette. The casemates would circumvallate the island, creating an impregnable and majestic façade, soaring and forbiddingly impressive to friend and foe alike. Projecting a medieval appearance, the citadel's gateway was to be located on the gorge side at the apex of the inverted "V" of the Rip Raps, fronting the main wharf.[60]

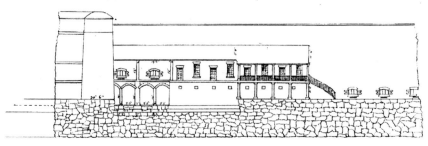

ELEVATION AND SECTIONS AT H I.

Side view of one of two barracks planned for the gorge side. View shows below-ground depth of foundation stone. Plan, 1864. *National Archives*.

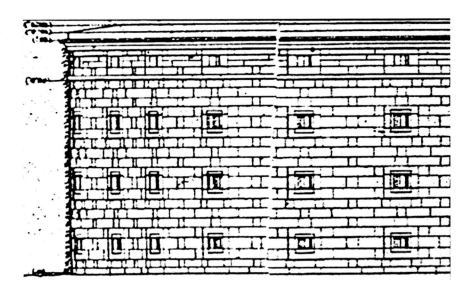

If finished according to the original plan, the formidable fort would have looked like this, four tiers high. Detail, plan. *National Archives*.

Andrew Jackson and his generation were well acquainted with earth- and wood-revetment fortifications, commonplace in the Creek Indian Wars and in the storied New Orleans defense. Fort Calhoun, however, was far more complex and enduring. It was granite, an extremely hard crystalline rock consisting mainly of feldspar and quartz, in color mostly gray to bluish gray, but occasionally pink, depending on where it was quarried.

Casemate interiors would consist of steel-gray slate floors, masonry walls, and brick ceilings. Load-bearing stone piers would support granite arches, themselves carrying the burden of both the barrel-vaulted brick ceilings and the outside walls. The barrel vaulting was a key component of the two lower tiers, the arched form providing further support for the tremendous weight of the casemates above. Directly underneath each such arch and beneath the flooring would be a reversed arch of brick, which spread the weight of the structure across the foundation. From inside the casemates, an observer would see an array of graceful arches.

The outside stone scarp or wall of both casemates and barbette would be fitted with embrasures, openings that allowed for cannon fire. Iron rails would be fastened to the floor as tracks for the artillery. Seacoast cannons mounted on wheeled carriages were designed to pivot to different firing positions within the angled embrasures.[61]

An integral part of the defense system was to be a boom raft, a removable obstruction intended to prevent the incursion of hostile vessels, extending across the channel between Old Point Comfort and the Rip Raps. A foundry

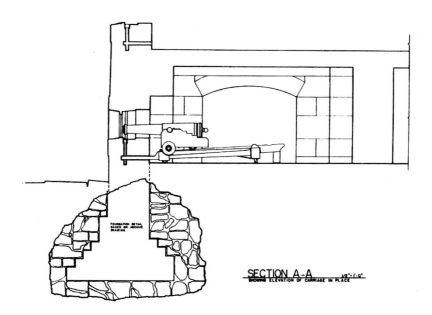

SECTION A-A

Drawing of gun carriage in place inside casemate, its barrel aimed through embrasure. Also shows load-bearing wall foundation deeply embedded into island stone. *Library of Congress.*

in West Point, New York, would be commissioned to manufacture 150 cast-iron anchors to secure the raft. As vital as it seemed to the planners, it was apparently never implemented.

By the fall of 1825, work on Fort Calhoun itself was underway. Manual cranes fashioned from oak and fitted with pivoted booms were mounted on red sandstone and sited primarily along the gorge side of the installation. The positioning of each boom was controlled by chains, sprockets, and gears. The workhorses of the operation, the cranes were used to offload watercraft delivering granite. Each building stone had a notch in the rock, which a crane could use to lift it. Then the material was hoisted onto a flatcar on a narrow-gauge railway, whence the load was moved across the work area to the point of construction or storage. Laborers pushed the cars and repositioned the rails when necessary. Cranes sited in the interior hoisted each stone into its final location.

The main wharf was vital to the reception of building material and supplies. It was substantial, long and wide in a fishhook shape, with heavy timber decking and supporting timbers driven into the sand.

White pine living quarters were built as soon as the elevation of the island was sufficiently above water for the safety of the men stationed there. Intended to provide basic accommodations, one for officers and others for soldiers and civilian workers, they were impermanent and scheduled to be demolished when the fort was completed. In yet another major brouhaha, the War Department reprimanded the engineers, finding the officers' quarters far more costly than originally anticipated. Accusations of impropriety were leveled, claiming a "permanent building of the same extent might be erected and handsomely finished for the sum which they have cost."

These quarters plus an office had been completed by late 1825. Two years later, additions included a carpenter shop, a mortar house, a blacksmith's

Tugboat, buffeted by turbulent waves in deep-water channel, passes the Rip Raps with buildings, cranes, and piles of stone now in evidence. Print, circa 1860.

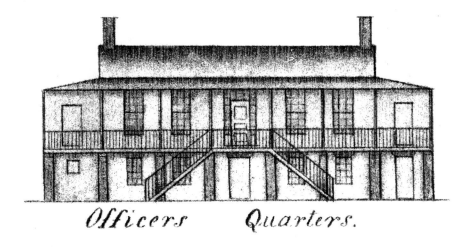

Officers Quarters.

Officers' quarters, deemed too sumptuous by Congressional inquiry. Presidents Jackson and Tyler stayed here, as did Robert E. Lee. Detail, Engineer Corps plan, 1826. *National Archives.*

shop, mechanic's quarters, a guardhouse, and a toolroom. The stone plane was surprisingly level, but wooden walkways nonetheless linked the buildings. Dirty floors were repeatedly swept with a hickory broom. Within the candlelit living quarters, the occupants slept on bunks with warmth provided by fireplaces. Shallow cisterns provided drinking water.[62]

A full two months after the dedication, stone was still being added to the Rip Raps. Masons could lay Fort Calhoun's stone walls only during low tide, probably because (as revealed by March 2007 excavations) the substantial granite foundation of the fort had been placed approximately ten feet below the surface. It was not until 1828 that Gratiot could report that matters had progressed to the point that work could be performed at all times. The initial tier of casemates would finally be erected during the following year.[63]

Both forts under construction were curiosities, attracting water excursions, a popular pastime of the day. In one such instance in late August 1828, passengers aboard the steamboat *Governor Wolcott*, out of Norfolk, felt that the "works of Old Point and the Rip Raps, the view of the Chesapeake Bay, and of the broad Atlantic, are objects [of] which [one] can never tire."[64]

Engineers used messengers to communicate their directives to workmen on various jobs in the far reaches of the Rip Raps. Ceaselessly occupied, these runners had to be sure-footed and diligent in order to traverse the

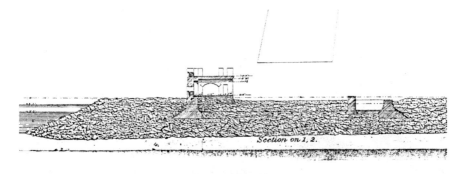

Drawing of casemate arch, demonstrating depth of large-stone foundation. Dotted lines indicate expected surface level and high-water level. Chief of Engineers plan, 1886. *National Archives.*

Archaeologist David K. Hazzard of Virginia Department of Historic Resources examines original Fort Calhoun foundation. Photograph, J. Michael Cobb, 2007.

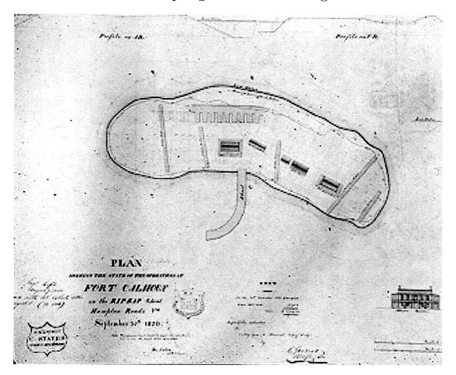

Engineer's plan of Fort Calhoun in September 1826, with first course of casemates underway, railways for moving stone, wharf, and building locations. *National Archives.*

cluttered surface or to scale rickety ladders. At times, a runner might encounter an impatient engineer seeking an immediate response or a sour and loud reaction to unpopular orders by a worker lacking the sand to meet the boss face to face.[65]

Top brass inspecting the construction's progress would also have to pick their way carefully about the Rip Raps. Although Fort Calhoun was intended to be a formidable citadel manned by the regular army, it was now filled with a motley crew of workingmen dressed in all manner of description, speaking the jargon and wielding the tools of their various crafts. This was the scene that Andrew Jackson encountered during his sojourns on the island.

Building the casemates was a daunting undertaking, requiring determination and training. Stonecutters shaped the granite blocks and the slate flooring for highly skilled masons who slapped on mortar and positioned the weighty pieces into the wall, the arches, or the floor, at times using a piece of slate to shim a given stone. Carpenters built wooden forms to support the brick barrel-vaulted ceilings until the mortar dried. Brick masons laid

Gently curved granite casemates as they appear today, demonstrating their simple geometric shapes, harmonious linear patterns, and intricate interlocking brickwork. Craftsmen worked here. Photograph, 2009. *David K. Hazzard.*

the vaults, with their often intricate intersections. Overseers looked over the men's shoulders to ensure that their jobs were performed properly.

The spring, summer, and fall were the working seasons. In the summer months, the water was warm and inviting. The granite generated intense heat, not unlike a stone frying pan, and with little cover provided from the sweltering sun men often plunged into the cool depths. Although the surrounding waters and a fairly constant breeze tempered the climate, the water boy was more than a welcome sight on exceedingly stifling days. Winter brought a stay of activity owing to cold winds whipsawing across the barren rock.

Laborers made up the greatest part of the contingent employed on the Rip Raps, varying in number from roughly twenty-five to sixty. Many hailed from eastern Virginia and other sections of the state, while some came from elsewhere. They were generally young men attracted to the project by steady government pay. At the beck and call of the overseer, a laborer was always busy. In general, he was tasked with the backbreaking drudgery of moving rock. Moreover, laborers gave a hand to the skilled craftsmen plying their trades. Turnover was not insignificant. More than a few were dismissed for a variety of infractions, while some found the work too hard and simply went away.[66]

Enslaved men were also forced to work on Fort Calhoun, and by 1860, as many as twenty-two slaves were involved in the undertaking. Slaveholders, chiefly from the environs of Hampton Roads, hired out the labor of the people they held in bondage. This was a legal transaction executed between the owner or the owner's agent and the government. Unlike the other laborers, enslaved people had no choice but to be there. Even though they were usually given the more difficult and dangerous jobs, some brought skills such as carpentry to the enterprise. One of those providing slave labor was Francis Anton Schmelz, a German immigrant and merchant in Hampton.[67]

Some men were hurt badly at this work, and a surgeon and a hospital steward were continuously posted on the Rip Raps. The transit of massive stone made crush injuries to body and limb probable. Mishandled sharp saws, planes, and chisels, misdirected hammer blows, and falls onto hard surfaces covered with stone fragments all took their toll. Physical injuries were common, including bone fractures, back ailments, and sprains. Heat-related stress and a variety of illnesses were also common, and some of the latter could be highly contagious among so many people in such a confined area.[68]

The blacksmith's shop was sweltering, noisy, and smoky. The small, open hut would have been cluttered with simple tools of the trade probably forged by the smith himself. With the aid of laborers, he made and repaired iron and steel objects needed for the fort's erection, including hardware for the buildings, nails, parts for the cranes, and chains. Metal was heated yellow-hot in the forge and, now pliable, was then picked up with tongs, hammered into form on the heavy anvil, and cooled in water. The difficult construction work took a great toll on workers' tools. The blacksmith spent a great deal of time repairing implements or making new ones.[69]

The tiresome and exacting project continued to progress, albeit slowly. By the time President Jackson found his way to the island, Fort Calhoun had realized less than half of Bernard's striking design. One course of casemates had been completed, and part of the second had been begun, while preliminary work had commenced on the gorge side. Even so, the fort was impressive.

And so it was found by Seba Smith, a satirical journalist who in August 1833 accompanied Andrew Jackson when the steamship *Columbia* was diverted to the Rip Raps from its normal Baltimore run. Smith's shrewd commentaries on the American scene were expressed under the nom de

Exterior view showing tightly fitted massive granite blocks, gun embrasures, and differently shaded granite. The fort never got higher than this. Photograph, 2009. *David K. Hazzard.*

plume "Major Jack Downing." He claimed to be struck by the "stupendous" fort taking shape and said he could not resist the temptation to jump off the *Columbia* to explore the "huge pile of stone." His comments on Castle Calhoun do not seem exaggerated. Viewing the surroundings, he

> *hurried with a quick step over the immense deposit of rock…not an inch of area had been reserved for a spear of grass, a shrub or a tree of any kind… great cranes are erected to elevate the stone to the desired level. These are furnished with ropes, chains, pulleys, and hooks, by which stones weighing more than a ton are carried from the water edge to the height of twenty feet.*

When finished, he judged that it would be a mighty bastion of the American republic.[70] However, the Rip Raps had taken on a forsaken semblance. Francis Blair, whose comments derive from the same visit, gave this assessment of a spot he would come to know well:

> *The present aspect of the place is rough and savage, and when the surge rushes in among the hollow piles of granite, and the wind whistles*

among the naked spars, which are planted round the walls for the support of the scaffolding, the music of the surrounding elements of sea and air...in keeping with the dreary, desolate spot, which, at a distance, looks like a Gibraltar beaten down by cannonade and fallen down prostrate in the sea.[71]

Chapter 6

DOSE OF HEATED GRANITE

T he year 1831 marked a significant transition in Fort Calhoun's evolution. Ominous signs began to materialize in the form of fissures in the stone piers and arches. The walls had risen in most places to the lintel stones that spanned the embrasures of the second tier. On November 4, Chief Engineer Gratiot informed Secretary of War Lewis Cass that, unexpectedly, the weight added by the fort's walls was causing a renewed settling of the Rip Raps.

Following this discovery, all construction on the battlement came to a halt. Gratiot also reported that loose stone and sand was being placed inside and outside the walls, as well as throughout the fort's interior. The goal was to redistribute the load so as to equalize the pressure on the sandy bottom of Hampton Roads and finish the settling process. While no one knew it at the time, the halt in construction would last nearly three decades. An engineer in 1953, having done borings at the site, said that the sand underlying the Rip Raps rocks was so deep that, had similar tests been done in 1818, it would probably not have been built at that location.[72]

Newly married to the granddaughter of George Washington's wife, twenty-four-year-old Second Lieutenant Robert E. Lee of the army's Engineer Corps brought his bride, Mary Custis, to Old Point Comfort in the spring of 1831, where, as his older brother Charles Carter Lee would write, "[H]e and his bride retreat to the walls and waves of Castle Calhoun." John C. Calhoun, at the end of his tenure at the War Department, had offered Lee an appointment to West Point, where he had graduated second in his class in 1829.[73]

Lee reported for duty to Andrew Talcott at Fort Monroe. Talcott, ten years older than Lee, was an established engineer. He had worked on fortifications on Lake Champlain and the upper Missouri and Yellowstone Rivers before coming to Hampton Roads. He later conducted construction improvements on the Dismal Swamp Canal.

Robert E. Lee. Portrait, William West, 1838. *Washington and Lee University.*

The two men became close friends, and their families saw much of one another. At first under Talcott's direction, and then alone, Lee would supervise the completion of Fort Monroe. He also strove to deal with the drawn-out settling process at Fort Calhoun. Owing to Talcott's protracted absences, Lee was often the engineer in charge. Like those that preceded him, Lee was responsible for dealing with the owners of scows carrying boulders to the island, and for inspecting the arriving materials. When additional building stone was required at Fort Monroe, he made use of

Andrew Talcott, in West Point uniform. Talcott became a Confederate colonel, designing fortifications for Richmond and the James River. Portrait, Thomas Sully, circa 1830. *Casemate Museum.*

rough-cut granite remnants from Fort Calhoun, which he could acquire for half the cost of material available elsewhere.[74]

Previously, Lee had served at the site of what would become Fort Pulaski on the Savannah River in Georgia. There he had been challenged with a situation much like the one at the Rip Raps: construction of a heavy fortification on an unstable foundation. Fort Pulaski was built on a sea of mud. Lee's daily task of supervising the placement of loadstone at Fort Calhoun was monotonous. An end-of-the-month report to Charles Gratiot one September was typical. Lee had done nothing but accept and distribute sand and stone. No change was anticipated in October.[75]

Inspections, often followed by reports, were also routine occurrences. The early summer of 1834 brought Secretary of War John Forsyth to view the "progress" of construction totally at a standstill. Soon thereafter, during sweltering July temperatures, curmudgeonly Inspector General of the Army Colonel John E. Wool arrived to have yet another look. Nettled by this redundancy, and two generations younger than the by-the-book traditionalist, Lee wrote to Talcott hoping that Wool would enjoy his "dose of heated granite."[76]

A bureaucratic dispute had been simmering over which branch of the army would oversee Fort Monroe's completion. Soon after the inspector general's visit, the War Department shifted command from the engineers to the Artillery Corps. Talcott was immediately ordered to New York to oversee defenses along the Hudson River. Miffed at this perceived affront to his professionalism, Talcott would soon resign his commission.

Lee was designated to work in the island's austere confines while living in the same officers' quarters in which the president of the United States periodically dwelled. Happy to remove himself from the bickering still reverberating between the engineers and the artillery contingent at Fort Monroe, Lee moved before his end-of-August reporting date, explaining, "I have commenced the 'residence' upon the Rip Raps and may be considered an old inhabitant."[77]

The engineer in charge frequently directed the use of small boats essential for work about the Rip Raps and for transport of men and material back and forth to Old Point Comfort. The vessels' importance to the work at Fort Calhoun is suggested by the construction of a boathouse and the large number of crewmen assigned to operate them. By October 1834, an "opening foundation for a boat house" was begun. Carpenters assisted by laborers raised the structure, located near the wharf. Each watercraft was manned with a coxswain and six boatmen. The boats received hard use, being regularly subjected to pounding waves and the angled edges of the rocks, and routinely underwent repairs and caulking.[78]

President Andrew Jackson contemplated fundamental changes, though we do not know exactly how he would have altered the citadel. Pressing to have it finished within the time remaining in his second term, as soon as the engineers would allow further work, Jackson apparently ordered alterations in its design. A frustrated Lee reported to Talcott that "[t]he President has played the Devil with the plan of Fort Calhoun." Lee sensed that completing the fort "[m]ight be too great a labor even for a Hercules." Trying to assuage the impatient and imperious president, Chief Engineer Gratiot claimed in his annual report that "its completion awaited only the firmness of the earth." "Firmness" was still in the future, however. No construction was to occur before Jackson left office in 1837.[79]

During the delays, alternative plans for the battlement were occasionally offered. One emanated from Joel Robert Poinsett, Martin Van Buren's secretary of war, who inspected Fort Calhoun in July 1837. He reported that the work "wears a melancholy, dilapidated appearance[.] [T]he evil is trifling now; but if neglected may become serious," because the subsidence was occurring unevenly and the scarp was bowing outward. He thought that "[i]t well may be necessary to bind the masonry together with iron bonds of great strength." Since the structure could not be permitted to rise farther until the settling finished, Poinsett thought that the existing first tier of casemates, and its top as a barbette, could be armed and used if necessary.[80]

Labor shortages, always a hindrance, became critical in the fall of 1838. The task of distributing loads of stone and sand was suspended on October 30, while the whole labor force was transferred over to Fort Monroe. On March 22, work resumed. As most available enslaved workmen were already engaged at the two forts, it was suggested to hire northern white wage labor for Fort Monroe and dispatch all the blacks to the Rip Raps, since that chore was considered to be much less desirable.[81]

The task of placing granite and sand to hasten subsidence ceased in December 1841. Engineers calculated that the island now supported a surplus of 13,627 tons of material over and above the fort's originally designed completion weight. Encouragingly, it was determined that the average rate of subsidence was decreasing. Engineers cautiously advised that the island should be allowed to settle for yet another year, which dragged into two, and in the winter of 1844, much to the dismay of the army, soundings indicated conclusively that the mass of stones was still subsiding. Compounding the problem, timber that had been utilized to equalize the positioning of the stone was decaying, and the immense weight of the granite was "pressing with great violence upon the piers." Work remained at a standstill as exasperated engineers continued to search for a solution.[82]

Meanwhile, Fort Calhoun once again became the alternative White House. John Tyler in April 1841 became the first vice president to assume the presidency when William Henry Harrison fell ill and died a month after his inauguration. Detractors called Tyler "His Accidency" and disputed

Stylized view, showing buildings, cranes, and piles of loadstone with which to settle the island. Engraving, *Harper's Weekly*, April 6, 1861. *William E. Rouse Research Library.*

whether he was really the chief executive, which took a heavy toll on him. Then, in September 1842, his wife Letitia died, and Tyler "took up his abode at the Rip Rap, for the purpose of seclusion and repose." He selected the retreat because of its isolation, and he was on familiar ground, having built his summer home Villa Margaret on the edge of nearby Hampton.[83]

Andrew Jackson, all too well acquainted with both the grief of losing a wife and the place Tyler had chosen for respite, expressed his deep sympathy. Responding, Tyler said gratefully, "The condition, in which I found myself plac'd by the death of the President elect, was one of immense difficulty and embarrassment...I shall at all times experience a lively satisfaction in hearing from you, and shall be flattered in receiving from you any suggestions relative to the conduct of public affairs." Tyler, like Jackson, performed his presidential duties and received friends at the Rip Raps. Senator Littleton Waller Tazewell of Norfolk visited his friend and colleague there. In early October 1842, the United States steamer *Poinsett* transported the Tyler family back to Washington.[84]

Tyler would be the last president to stay in those quarters. Fire raced through the president's house on the Rip Raps in the morning hours of April 18, 1846. Colonel Rene E. DeRussy of Fort Monroe was awakened by a fire alarm, and to prevent the blaze from spreading, he and his men demolished the wooden gangways connecting the other buildings, which they were able to save. DeRussy reported: "I regret to state that the building formerly occupied by Presidents Jackson and Tyler is consumed to its foundations."[85]

John Tyler. Photograph of print, circa 1860. *Library of Congress.*

Fort Wool

Martin Van Buren, William Henry Harrison, John Tyler, James K. Polk, and Zachary Taylor all served in the presidency during the decade of the 1840s. Over the same ten-year period, the Republic of Texas was annexed, the Mexican-American War was waged, and the northern third of Mexico was ceded to the United States. The telegraph and the sewing machine were invented, and gold was discovered in California. While industrialization took firm hold of the nation's production, and American territory was significantly expanded, progress at Fort Calhoun remained at a virtual standstill.

During the succeeding decade, many innovations in military architecture and technology occurred. Larger magazines, more up-to-date armament, and Totten embrasures were incorporated into Fort Calhoun's design. Invented by Army Chief of Engineers Brigadier General Joseph Totten, the new embrasures consisted of wrought-iron shutters that could be fitted into the existing cannon portals, designed to protect artillerymen and guns. The originally open embrasures, termed "murderous funnels," were susceptible to enemy fire.

Fort Wool has some fine examples of Totten embrasures. In an interior view of an unfinished casemate, its doors are open. Photograph, 2009. *David K. Hazzard.*

Star-Spangled Banner Rising

At long last, toward the end of 1857, Colonel DeRussy decided that the prolonged settling period had passed. The Rip Raps had stabilized and was ready to bear the full load of the structures. In the winter of 1858, granite blocks were placed in readiness to complete the second course of casemates. On May 17, DeRussy could state that the load-bearing piers were being made level in preparation for the new masonry. The wharf was upgraded, cranes and derricks were erected by the carpenters and laborers, and machinery was being repaired.

Once begun, work proceeded rapidly, as though the island were disgusted by the long abeyance and thirsted for new stone. By June 1859, cracks and gaps in the first course had been repaired, and by December industrious masons were adding to the stones of the second tier. They were also preparing stone blocks for the third tier. In addition, the embrasures in the first tier were being refitted for the Totten iron shutters, while blacksmiths were turning out the bolts for the shutter frames. All the while, the chore of removing the loadstone dragged on; most of it was dropped overboard.

DeRussy reported the next month that the masons were finishing the second tier and commencing work on the third. The new mortar shed was well underway, while the blacksmith shop was forging the hinges for its doors. Laborers were occupied with whitewashing the quarters and storehouse. Carpenters were tasked with remaking the lumber house and putting a fence around it. Other assignments included grading the parade ground and painting the privies in the rear of the barracks.

In the public eye, however, the great promise of Fort Calhoun had faded over the long settling period. Even now with the frenzy of renewed effort, the luster and glory of realizing Bernard's grand scheme seemed to have passed. The memory of the 1812 outrage had dimmed, no new invaders threatened, the United States had become a forceful hemispheric power rather than being a hesitant shrinking violet, and it seemed to many that the rock castle at the mouth of Hampton Roads was an endless error rather than a necessary defense mechanism. Benson J. Lossing, an editor and popular historian whose interests ranged broadly, mentioned in passing in his widely read history of the Revolution that "it is to be hoped that not another hour will be employed upon [Fort Calhoun], except to carry away the stones for the more useful and more noble purpose of erecting an iron-foundry or a cotton-mill." The *New York World* on August 7, 1860, reported the fortification as being

> [a] *heterogeneous mass of hewn blocks of stone, at present without apparent form or comeliness... Topped off with derricks and tenements for workmen,*

it looks at this distance like a hermitage for criminals, the inmates of which, after a life of recreation with the stone hammer, are to expiate their still unexpiated offenses by the agency of the hangman. Forty-one years ago the first cargo of stone for that fort was thrown over in eighteen fathoms of water, on the spot where the pile is now [still] *being slowly reared.*[86]

Chapter 7

FEARFUL HAVOC

The sectional crisis was now moving toward secession by the slave states, and civil war. Seemingly overnight, Fort Calhoun became important, busy, and militarily active.

More than a few of the men working on the construction at Fort Calhoun were secessionist or soon would be. William J. Stores, reared nearby in Elizabeth City County, was typical. Billy had attended Hampton Academy, where, as a recently instituted part of the curriculum, he and other young men received military training in preparation for war with the North. Although he probably had a laborer's job on the Rip Raps, when the war came, Billy joined the Confederate army in May 1861 as an officer.[87]

The Confederacy's newly installed Jefferson Davis administration nullified Federal law and proclaimed the confiscation of government property. It viewed the occupation of Forts Monroe and Calhoun as a transgression of Virginia's sovereignty. Meanwhile, Union army General-in-Chief Winfield Scott in the spring of 1861 made Fort Monroe's reinforcement a paramount objective. Scott understood that holding Fort Monroe was the key to suppressing the rebellion in Virginia, the Confederacy's most influential state. Abraham Lincoln rejected the constitutional legitimacy of secession and was determined to "hold, and occupy, and possess the property and places belonging to the government." With Scott's reinforcements, Fort Monroe became impregnable to Southern attack, and both forts remained in Union hands during the entire conflict.[88]

Former president John Tyler chaired the February 1861 Washington Peace Conference. It was a forlorn attempt to save the Union. Tyler, really in favor of secession anyhow, declared that "the specter of war had arrived" when the garrison at Fort Monroe swiveled one of its mighty guns landward, looming over the "sacred soil of Virginia." Upon the Old Dominion's vote for

William "Billy" Stores in Confederate military uniform. Ambrotype, C.R. Rees & Co., Richmond, circa 1861.

In the mid-1850s, German artist Edward Beyer rendered from Fort Calhoun this idyllic view of Old Point Comfort, with riprap stone in foreground. Lithograph. *William E. Rouse Research Library.*

secession in April, Tyler wrote his second wife Julia, "Well, my dearest one, Virginia has severed her connection with the Northern hive of abolitionists, and takes her stand as a sovereign and independent State…to resume the powers she had granted the Federal government, and to stand before the world clothed in the full vestments of sovereignty." The Union's continuing possession of Tyler's earlier retreat, Fort Calhoun, and its companion Fort Monroe were tests of the validity of the state's sovereignty.[89]

Winfield Scott had received in January a report on the state of readiness of all Federal fortifications. Those in Charleston, South Carolina, had already fallen to Confederate forces, so lines were slashed through the entry for Fort Sumter, which had been greatly strengthened before it was surrendered. Its companion, Fort Moultrie, was said to have been "in the best condition possible under the circumstances prior to its evacuation." In Hampton Roads, Fort Monroe was declared to be in "[e]xcellent defensible condition—needs minor repairs only." Despite all the recent flurry of activity, Fort Calhoun was gloomily listed as "[u]nder construction. Not ready for armament or garrison."[90]

In July 1861, Fort Calhoun was plainly not equipped for the coming hostilities. Nine masons, assisted by nineteen laborers, were busy working on the rising granite edifice. Not a single piece of artillery projected from a casemate. The urgency of the situation was realized, and the War Department rushed to garrison and arm the fort. By September, Captain C. Seaforth Stewart could inform his superior in the Engineers Corps, Joseph Totten, that seven eight-inch Columbiad cannons were mounted in the casemates. Four were placed on the crucial west end of the island fronting

The huge concentration of Union forces at Camp Hamilton, with many tents and barracks. Fort Monroe, transport ships are visible (rear). Lithograph, Casimir Bohn, 1862.

the roadstead and the Confederate forces gathering on the Norfolk shore, at Sewell's Point, while the remaining guns were mounted on the eastern end of the Rip Raps to guard the channel entrance. Additional armament included two forty-two-pound guns probably mounted on the second tier. The fort's most effective weapon, a rifled Sawyer gun, was positioned on the wharf with its muzzle directed at Sewell's Point.[91]

Scott's specific instructions to Major General Benjamin F. Butler, the new commandant of Forts Monroe and Calhoun, were to thwart the Confederates from mounting artillery at Sewell's Point. Rebel batteries to the south at Craney Island and any others in the vicinity were also to be taken. Troops massed at Sewell's Point could threaten the Union forts, while enemy artillery positions could harass Union shipping. Butler was further encouraged to recapture the Gosport Navy Yard. To realize these objectives, Butler and the commander of the naval forces would need to act together.[92]

Five days after his appointment, on May 27, 1861, Butler moved two thousand troops to Newport News, across the end of the peninsula on which Fort Monroe sat. An entrenched camp named for Butler was established on high ground at the mouth of the James River. Four eight-inch Columbiads were mounted, providing a threat to the Confederate position at Craney Island.[93]

Above: Mounted on second tier, cannons are futilely discharged toward Sewell's Point, while cranes, stones, and uninstalled granite blocks stand idle. Print, circa 1861.

Right: Benjamin F. Butler. Engraving, *Pictorial Battles of the Civil War*, 1885.

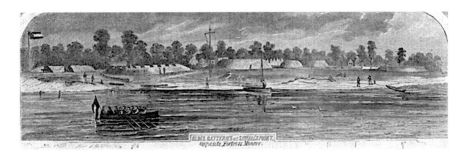

Confederate batteries mounting thirty guns at Sewell's Point, partially obscured by trees. *Harper's Weekly*, November 2, 1861.

Even with Camp Butler, the Rip Raps was the furthermost land-fixed projection of Union firepower in Hampton Roads. The major threat to Fort Calhoun was the developing Confederate stronghold at Sewell's Point, about three miles away.

A Union report on the Rebels' fortifications noted their strength: "The works are well constructed, supplied with magazines, many contain[ing] powder and loaded shells; also bombproof traverses and store rooms, and along the line are found furnaces for heating shot." Clearly worried about Fort Calhoun's firepower, the Rebels were attempting to anchor their right flank with a battery for four guns, completely hidden by wood and brush from the water side. "This battery is much nearer the Rip Raps, which it fronts and commands, and might have proved very annoying if the guns had been in position." Another battery about a mile to the left mounted two rifled eighty-pounders, while nearby stood yet another battery armed with three smoothbore guns. The chief fortification on the point was a "well-built earth fort, having bastioned flanks, with a redan in front. It has commodious barracks and officers' quarters and a parade ground." Thirty-three guns of various types were placed here. The cannoneers at the Rip Raps and Sewell's Point became nemeses.[94]

The Sawyer Rifle at Fort Calhoun could reach Sewell's Point. Invented by Sylvanus Sawyer, improvements to the gun's projectiles were patented in 1855 and tested at the island fortification. On a pleasant day, June 15, 1861, Sawyer and Butler tried out the weapon against Sewell's Point. With Butler observing aboard a steamer, the gun's deadly shells mostly passed over the distant earthworks. However, some hit, making "the Johnnies scatter." It was said that one projectile "passed close to a house, and the inmates ran up a white flag." Fort Calhoun was at last engaged in actual warfare, although its shots went neither in the direction nor against the kind of enemy that had been imagined in its inception.[95]

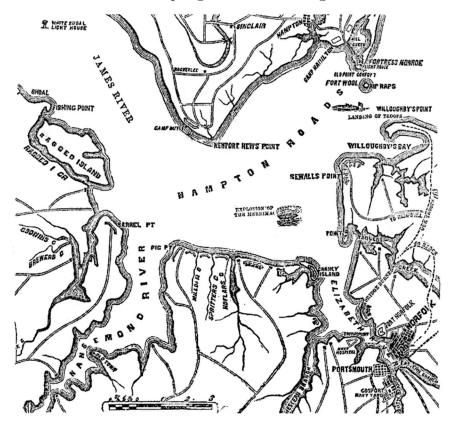

Civil War map showing Camp Butler, Camp Hamilton, Norfolk invasion site, Sewell's Point batteries, site of *Virginia* scuttling, and Craney Island. *Philadelphia Inquirer*, May 12, 1862.

Under this barrage, Augusta Jane Evans felt the Sawyer Rifle's effects while visiting Georgia soldiers encamped at Sewell's Point: "The immense Rifled cannon at the Rip Raps thundered angrily…and a heavy shell exploded a few yards from us. I turned my glass at once at the Rip Raps, and distinctly saw the muzzle of the villainous gun." Evans, a popular Southern author, then saw the gunners reloading to send their "missile of death right at us. Oh! I longed for a secession flag to shake defiantly in their teeth at every fire!"[96]

On June 20, Butler reported to Winfield Scott that the efforts were successful. The *National Intelligencer* exulted: "An experiment with Sawyer's American Rifle cannon at the Rip Raps last evening was a brilliant success. Sewell's Point is clearly within range of this tremendous projectile. Seven of the eleven 48-pound shells exploded a short distance from the rebel camp, one of them over their entrenchment." Thereafter, Captain Alexander B.

Officers watch as lanyard is pulled, Fort Calhoun's Sawyer Rifle belches shell skyward toward Sewell's Point. Flagman relays outcome. *Frank Leslie's Illustrated Newspaper*, August 31, 1861.

Dyer, arsenal commander at Fort Monroe and later chief of army ordnance, experimented with the James and Hotchkiss rifled guns from the Fort Calhoun wharf, but only the Sawyer Rifle had sufficient range to reach Sewell's Point. There was, however, the problem of directing fire accurately against the Rebel stronghold.[97]

Owing to the Rebels' clever use of trees, their fortifications at Sewell's Point were virtually obscured from the direct sight of the Union gunners. Aerial reconnaissance helped. Having conducted several trial ascensions from Hampton in his hot air balloon, John La Mountain undertook his first military aerial observations, on July 31 from the land (in Hampton), and on August 3 from the waters near the island. The armed transport *Fanny* was used to convey La Mountain and his balloon into Hampton Roads opposite Sewell's Point. The aeronaut then rose two thousand feet to observe the enemy works. He saw slaves and freedmen laboring to erect the new fortifications for artillery designed to threaten the Rip Raps and United States shipping. These ascensions formed the first effective balloon reconnaissance by the United States Army.[98]

John La Mountain's balloon *Atlantic* makes anchored ascension near Old Point to observe Confederate positions in Hampton Roads. *Frank Leslie's Illustrated Newspaper*, August 31, 1861.

But accuracy in fire demanded more. Artillerymen at the Sawyer Rifle needed to know the effect of their fire. This convinced Major Albert J. Myer that the time had arrived to test his new signaling system. The Signal Corps had a school of instruction at Fort Monroe led by Myer, the army's first chief signal officer, who had devised a system of signaling across long distances using a single flag (or one lantern or torch at night), waved back and forth in a code known as "wig-wag" signaling or aerial telegraphy.

Myer and several other officers aboard a tugboat just out of range of the Sewell's Point guns observed the shelling of the Rebel position. They became the center point of a signal flag network linking gunboats in Hampton Roads with Forts Calhoun and Monroe. Myer's group was able to report hits, misses, and corrections back by flag to gun battery officers at the Rip Raps. This was one of the earliest uses of communication by flag signaling during the Civil War.[99]

In late August, with Ben Butler and the visiting General John Wool observing, and with Myer signaling, the Sawyer Rifle commenced firing once again. Its second shell exploded in the midst of the Rebel camp, breaking the flagstaff and "scatter[ing] the rebels like chaff." The Rip Raps troops continued to fire with great accuracy and made fearful havoc within the Confederate batteries, even though protection had been given to their gun

Onlookers on Fort Calhoun's wharf including Generals Wool and Butler, who observe firing of Sawyer Rifle toward Sewell's Point three miles distant. Engraving, *Official War Record*, 1898.

emplacements by covering them with iron railroad ties. Another account reported that a "secesh" steamer appeared and, upon the firing, immediately whirled around.[100]

Sporadic exchanges of artillery fire would occur between the Rip Raps and Sewell's Point thereafter, until Union forces captured Norfolk later in the conflict. However, no damage was ever inflicted on the island castle from these exchanges.

Fort Calhoun was vulnerable to a Confederate assault from Sewell's Point after dark, even with the proximity of Fort Monroe and the guns of the Union fleet. The *Anacostia* was assigned the mission of watching Sewell's Point to warn the fleet of approaching fire rafts or floating torpedoes. Captain William B. Alexander, in early June 1861, was dispatched with twenty members of the Twenty-third Massachusetts Regiment to take command of the Rip Raps, with orders to prevent any "rebels from landing here."

Eighty men attached to Bartlett's Naval Brigade were already present on the island, along with a throng of stonemasons and laborers. Captain Alexander found life easy there, with "very good quarters I have a room to myself and do as I have a mind to." Alluding to mail delivery, Alexander remarked that every morning a boat was sent to Fort Monroe to pick it up. He was confident it would be a "magnificent fort when it was done."[101]

Interservice rivalries existed even in this time of extreme emergency for the Union. In mid-October, as Fort Calhoun was surrounded by water, military officials considered placing the navy in charge of the guns and batteries on the island under the leadership of Commodore Louis M. Goldsborough, commander of the North Atlantic Blockading Squadron. Goldsborough, anxious to strengthen the citadel and clear away its rocky construction debris to make it more ready for war, stated:

> *The enemy is evidently very busy in making preparations for a blow here abouts, and the Rip Raps should be placed in good fighting order forthwith. It is far from being in such a state now...the main thing is to get the place cleared away and prepared, to have guns mounted as rapidly as possible, and then to have the right sort of men on hand to fight them.*

Apparently, the transition of the fort's batteries from the army to the navy was never fulfilled.[102]

Naval action, however, provided the next military encounter for Fort Calhoun. Both sides had hurried to complete ironclad warships. At the Gosport Navy Yard, the Confederates refitted the *Merrimack* into the *Virginia*. The newly iron-plated warship ventured out of the Elizabeth River into Hampton Roads on March 8, 1862, a clear day with the water like glass. In support, the Confederate battery at Sewell's Point commenced firing on the Union fleet. The artillerymen at the Rip Raps returned the fire toward Sewell's Point with the Sawyer Rifle, while turning the Columbiads against the Rebel ironclad. The *Virginia* was too far away for the shelling to have any damaging effect, and it undertook the task of assailing several wooden ships of the Union fleet positioned off Camp Butler. The *Virginia* rammed the twenty-four-gun sloop *Cumberland* before exchanging fire and setting the fifty-gun frigate *Congress* afire. Both sank as Rebel onlookers cheered and Union sympathizers were dismayed.[103]

Minnesota, Roanoke, and *St. Lawrence* were approaching to join the fray, but disheartened by *Virginia's* startling success, they withdrew toward shallow water, where they hoped that *Virginia's* deep draft would protect them. In disarray, all three gunboats stranded themselves on Middle Ground shoal. While *Roanoke* and *St. Lawrence* managed to reach the protection of Fort Monroe's guns, *Minnesota* remained aground. The Union navy had been swiftly and abjectly defeated, with almost 250 casualties and the loss of two

Confederates shout encouragement as *Virginia* steams past Sewell's Point batteries to battle in Hampton Roads. Engraving, *Battles and Leaders of the Civil War*, 1884.

Seen from Newport News Point, *Cumberland*'s injured are carried off, while *Monitor* and *Virginia* blaze away. Camp Butler at right. Lithograph, Kurz and Allison, 1889.

major armed ships. This encounter was unquestionably devastating, one of the worst defeats suffered by the United States Navy.

That night, through the dreadful hours of darkness, the garrisons on the Rip Raps and at Fort Monroe exchanged signals continually. Fort Monroe was chaotic: "[F]erries, gunboats, and tugboats came and went in all directions; drums and bugles were beating and ringing with unwonted ardor." Union ships in the vicinity prepared to run for the open sea if the *Virginia* were to approach. Fatefully, however, the North's ironclad *Monitor* arrived from New York City that evening. On the island, the New Yorkers of the Naval Brigade stood by their guns, realizing that the outcome of the war might depend on the next day's action. "Thus dawned the day of the 9th of March. Early we were grouped on the parapet around our cannons, spying eagerly toward Sewell's Point and the *Minnesota*, yet veiled by a light fog."[104]

In an attempt to renew its good work from the previous day, *Virginia*, mounting eight eleven-inch guns, made its way into Hampton Roads as the *Monitor*, equipped with its rotating turret and two eleven-inch Dahlgren guns, moved into position to protect the immobile *Minnesota*, and the epic duel commenced. As the armor-clad vessels pounded each other with shells at short range for nearly four hours, their heavily plated sides averted any significant damage. In their initial encounter, the two harbingers of naval warfare to come would battle to a draw. The artillerymen on Castle Calhoun used their guns to keep *Virginia* away from the exit to Hampton Roads and desultorily fired on the Rebel ironclad every time it seemed sufficiently close. The mood of the soldiers changed from depression to exultation as they watched and cheered their countrymen manning *Monitor*.[105]

Virginia was now bottled up inside Hampton Roads, thanks to *Monitor* and the two guardian fortifications, but it still continued its threatening patrols, and Fort Calhoun continued to fire at it, with two shots on April 11 and another on May 8. Sewell's Point and the Rip Raps persisted in their back-and-forth duel, one of the shots from the Sawyer Rifle "filled with the new liquid fire explod[ing] in the midst of the rebel parade grounds."[106]

Edgy and wary about the prowling *Virginia*, Lieutenant Colonel Gustav B. Helleday, in command on the island, reported on April 26, 1862, that small boats were seen near Sewell's Point during the day and, along with floating lights, at night. The enemy was busy sounding the channel. "A gunboat might destroy these buoys, or whatever they are." Nothing apparently became of these Rebel activities.[107]

As usually happens in wartime, people who wanted to make a buck flocked to the battlefront. Across the channel at Old Point Comfort, a multitude of sutlers, men and women, began to gather "almighty coppers,

The battle of the *Monitor* and the *Virginia*. Lithograph, Calvert Lithograph Co., 1891. *Library of Congress*.

Soldiers on Rip Raps (left) had a good view of the ironclads and the Union sailors cowering under Fort Monroe's guns. *Harper's Weekly*, April 12, 1862.

from the pestilential camp and the reeking battlefield." They built rough plank shanties on the strand surrounding Fort Monroe. Many were masters of sloops or schooners bearing freight from New York and Baltimore to Old Point. They trafficked in every "necessity or luxury," sending wagons to the outlying camps. A February 1862 *New York Herald* article reported: "Any sutler or dealer detected in selling liquor is sent out of the department, or granted a short residence at the fashionable resort of rogues, officially known as Fort Calhoun, vulgarly as Rip Raps."[108]

The Rip Raps was an exciting spot from which to view the unfolding war in Hampton Roads. Vessels were steadily plying through the channel. From the ramparts of Fort Calhoun, the men witnessed the impressive pageant of the arrival of General George B. McClellan's Army of the Potomac from the port of Alexandria, in preparation for a major drive on the Confederate capital at Richmond, ninety-odd miles to the west. In the spring of 1862, a civilian flotilla of almost four hundred vessels shuttled the troops to Fort Monroe. The fleet included everything from Long Island side-wheelers and Hudson River excursion boats to Philadelphia ferryboats. The Union army of 121,500 soldiers flowed into area camps located on land captured from

Generals Butler and Wool observe the firing of the famous "Union" gun, on the beach near Fort Monroe. *New York Illustrated News*, September 9, 1861.

Old Point, with the Hygeia Hotel in front of Fort Monroe, and soldiers disembarking on the wharf. Engraving, 1861.

the Rebels. "We arrived safe at Fort Monroe when a site [*sic*] met our eyes that put us in the mind of New York. Ships were here in swarms," recalled a New Jersey soldier describing the vast panorama of tall-masted vessels.[109]

Across the channel from "the low walls and black derricks" of Fort Calhoun, the massive army spread out on the shoreline formed part of a memorable spectacle. Along with the Old Point Comfort Lighthouse and the Hygeia Hotel, one could see an assortment of military buildings including barracks, hospitals, wharves, stables, and a signal station. Soldiers crowded into Kimberly Brothers store for tobacco and other personal items or, when time allowed, searched leisurely for oysters. The massive "Union" and "Lincoln" guns stood steadfast on the beach, arrayed for battle with the *Virginia*. Itinerant Northern journalist George A. Townsend wrote:

> *The bar at the Hygeia House was beset with thirsty and idle people, who swore instinctively, and drank raw spirits passionately. The quantity of shell, ball, ordnance, camp equipage, and war munitions of every description piled around the fort, was marvelously great…Energy and enterprise displayed their implements of death on every hand.*[110]

Chapter 8

SOFT TIMES

Ben Butler, standing on the Rip Raps amidst the terrible machinery of internecine warfare, was no doubt mindful of Andrew Jackson's one-time presence there and his own efforts to hold the Union together. Butler had come of age in the nationalist shadow cast by Andrew Jackson. His father, Captain John Butler, had been a bearer of dispatches for Old Hickory at the Battle of New Orleans. John would name his first son Andrew Jackson Butler, and Ben as a young man had been dazzled "with the brilliancy of Jackson's administration of national affairs." Butler proved to be almost as brilliant, emulating the decisiveness of his family's hero in administering the rebellious population of the ever-increasing areas formerly in the Confederacy that came under his control.[111]

Jackson's and Butler's devotion to the Union was shared by common soldiers, but cares about good governance were remote. Garrison life and soldierly duties at the Rip Raps early in the war were fairly easy and light. Troops attached to the Twenty-ninth Massachusetts Regiment were the first to be posted on the "little island," consisting of Captain Israel Wilson's Company B and Captain Lebbeus Leech's Company C. The men and boys from the region around Marblehead were accustomed to a maritime environment. In the summer of 1861, they were tasked with mounting the cumbersome Columbiad cannons in the casemates, a chore the men detested. Another bane of a soldier's existence, the repetitive and monotonous parade drill, was limited here because buildings, cranes, the granite for the casemates, and piles of loadstone crowded the parade ground. Hours were devoted to cleaning weapons, spit-shining brass insignia, and caring for equipage. They lived in the existing temporary structures, though perhaps some used tents.

These were "soft times," as men sent and received letters from home. Illicit alcohol and games of chance were commonplace. They caught plenty

Ships under sail and steam churn the busy channel between the Rip Raps and Old Point Comfort as portrayed in *Harper's Weekly*, June 22, 1861.

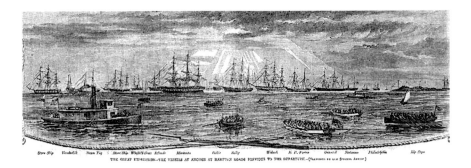

The Great Naval Expedition to Port Royal, South Carolina, comprises seventy-seven vessels and is assembled near the Rip Raps (right). *Harper's Weekly*, October 1861.

of fish, oysters, and crabs, and they swam around the wharf. Enlisted men, whiling away the day about the rocks, shared endless stories and opinions of politics, women left behind, and military movements, while hours were spent discussing "gravely the situation of the country, planning campaigns, and fighting imaginary battles."[112]

At nightfall, the Rip Raps appeared as a hazy, ghostly silhouette. On the fort, lantern light distorted the forms of men and buildings, which from a distance could be both eerie and comforting. In late March 1862, with the menacing *Virginia* able to approach within range of the Rip Raps, lights at night would be prohibited, cloaking the island in pitch blackness. Voices of sentries carried over the water. Sometimes fog rolled in, and vessels were forced to use their horns. With extremely thick fog, day or night, it was impossible to see beyond a few yards off the rocks. At times, the dark shape of the island could be discerned only by a sharp eye.

Union Naval Brigade celebrating with cannon fireworks on the Fourth of July at Fort Monroe. *Harper's Weekly*, July 27, 1861. *William E. Rouse Research Library.*

On November 3, 1861, two companies of the Ninety-ninth New York, then under the command of Colonel Washington A. Bartlett, became Fort Calhoun's complement, relieving the Massachusetts troops. Two of its companies remained at Fort Monroe. This hard-luck regiment of former sailors had originally been organized in New York City. It called itself Bartlett's Naval Brigade since it was planned to serve on gunboats. The New Yorkers arrived in Virginia with no weapons or uniforms. Got up by Butler in flannel shirts, white duck pants, and straw hats and provided with arms, the troublesome men took their places on the Rip Raps.[113]

The men of the Ninety-ninth were ordered by General Butler to continue the process of mounting the Columbiads at night, when they would have more protection. While supervising this operation, Bartlett, probably more than slightly lubricated, fell from the top of a casemate and sustained a nearly fatal injury. Gustav Helleday succeeded Bartlett in command. Following this accident and the departure of several field officers who were disgusted with Butler's strict and unyielding regime, the regiment became demoralized. Butler reorganized the outfit as the Union Coast Guard, and the two island companies constituted the Fort Wool garrison throughout most of 1862.[114]

Every Sunday morning, first sergeants inspected the troops' barracks and arms, and each day at 8:00 a.m. they paraded in dress uniform on the wharf for lack of space on the parade ground. They were forbidden the random discharge of arms but were allowed target practice under officers' supervision. Captain Richard Nixon was ordered to supervise the landing of steamboats at the dock, "to see that it is not injured," since winds and swift currents often dashed vessels against it. They were joined on June 8, 1862, by Company A of the Eighth New York Militia.[115]

Persons other than workers and soldiers were on the crowded island. Some were placed there for purposes of punishment, while many saw freedom in the rocks. In May 1861, while engaged in erecting Confederate fortifications at Sewell's Point, three enslaved men belonging to Hamptonian Francis King Mallory—Frank Baker, Shepard Mallory, and James Townsend—had made the fateful decision to flee their bondage. They clandestinely traveled by boat to Hampton and then on to Fort Monroe. Butler, an astute lawyer, had concluded that the three were "contraband of war" under international law because they were property being used for military purposes. The decision was a military necessity, as he explained to General Scott. The Sewell's Point batteries threatened Butler's naval operations in the roadstead. His action deprived the enemy of its labor force and at the same time supplied Butler with sorely needed workers. Soon thereafter, hundreds and then thousands of men, women, and children streamed to "Freedom's Fort."[116]

The Rip Raps offered liberty, too, being much closer to and in plain sight of Sewell's Point, which made it a convenient haven for fugitives. It is not difficult to imagine enslaved men with shovels in hand looking over freshly turned dirt toward the Union-held island with its flag of liberty barely discernable, thinking that freedom was very close. Indeed, they did not have to make the perilous channel crossing in open boats. Black hands in the night could reach out from the water to climb on the rocks and for the first time feel a sense of liberty. On one day alone in late October 1861, eleven enslaved men arrived at Fort Calhoun from Sewell's Point. The newcomers eagerly related everything they knew about the Rebel ramparts.[117]

After all, the fort was well known to enslaved persons in eastern Virginia, part of their collective memory and experience. For some, generations of their families had toiled on the rocks or at Old Point. One such gentleman, now transformed into contraband, told a Massachusetts soldier near Fort Monroe that he remembered often seeing Andrew Jackson and Francis Blair at the Rip Raps.[118]

Soldiers thought of the Rip Raps as a prison, and for some it was designated as a place of punishment. Moss Specht from Beavertown, Pennsylvania, noted: "When they arrest deserters or any other soldiers deserving harsh punishment they are taken there." According to General Wool, it was "the only place we have for prisoners of war and convicts." Some were critical of the "incongruous association of sailors, soldiers and convicts," but they were disregarded. By October 1861, perhaps sixty prisoners were held in the makeshift prison.[119]

Ben Butler, when confronted with disobedience among New York's Hawkins Zouaves, found the Rip Raps a convenient place to secure the dissidents. The men refused to obey orders and wanted to return to their homes. They were aggrieved that they had not been paid, were dissatisfied with their officers, thought they had not been regularly mustered into the army, and were given bad food. About twelve ringleaders were sent to Fort Calhoun. The troops stationed there were sympathetic to their comrades and treated them kindly.

Charles Johnson, one of the Hawkins mutineers, made the most of his confinement. Surrounded by water, the prisoners were provided with quarters and were not restrained but permitted to wander freely. Johnson saw the construction workers engaged in a task, "though exactly what I could not discover." He made use of the "not inconsiderable" library and perused some of Frederica Bremer's work. Impressed with the island's armament, Johnson made a sketch of one of the seacoast guns mounted in a casemate, aimed at Sewell's Point, depicting the "solidity and massiveness of these walls." His curiosity was roused by the discovery of an old cannon barrel embedded in the riprap stone, probably used to tie off incoming vessels or to secure crane guy lines. He also made a rendering of the *Minnesota*, the flagship of the North Atlantic Squadron, which he saw in the channel off the island.

Johnson's drawing of a casemate cannon, including the track on which the gun pivoted for firing. *The Long Roll*, 1911.

FORT WOOL

Johnson framed the *Minnesota* with the rocks of the Rip Raps, and Fort Monroe in the background. *The Long Roll*, 1911.

Gazing into the briny depths, Johnson observed the jellyfish,

> *those beautiful creatures we had watched with great pleasure, as with their slow methodical motions, they propelled themselves about the island, which seemed to them a favorite resort, for nowhere else have I seen them in such beautiful variety and so numerous.*

Johnson had a somewhat Jacksonesque episode, "not so terrible as an affair with a shark," but it was bad enough. He was "seized by a legion of little devils with pins in them…on every part of my body under water, they clung, pricking, biting, sucking and stinging." Enduring great agony, he hurried toward the dock. Despite his nettle adventure, this contented prisoner experienced

> *many a delightful day spent among the Rip Rap rocks, writing, reading and drawing; the ever-varying and shifting scenes of an important naval and military station in a time of war, continually furnishing new objects of interest to a mind somewhat alive to beauties of nature, I enjoyed everything to the utmost.*[120]

Star-Spangled Banner Rising

In the aftermath of General Ambrose Burnside's Cape Hatteras Expedition to North Carolina, perhaps forty prisoners resided there. Civilians were also imprisoned on the Rip Raps, almost always without the benefit of a trial. Common offenses were disloyalty—which could range from spying to disrespecting Federal orders or the symbols of Union authority—and purveying contraband goods. Not unexpectedly, noncombatant prisoners were discontented (two of them had died), lamenting, "We cannot realize that the Government of the United States thus refuses us our liberty, wastes our property and places our persons on this island of rock that we may by cruelty and oppression be taught to hate the Government under which we were born." So a committee representing over one hundred civilian inmates wrote on July 4, 1862, to General George B. McClellan. Some hailed from local counties, and others were from distant places. They petitioned against arbitrary arrest and detention "without a change of clothes" and were "now covered with vermin of this prison house…They are without funds with which they can procure the necessaries or comforts with which to promote cleanliness or preserve health." They also feared that "our slaves have left us; that our household furniture has been wantonly destroyed…and that our growing crops have been wasted…our homes except for the presence of loved wives and children are barren deserts."

Brigadier General Joseph K.F. Mansfield, who sent many of the men to the island, was not moved by their alleged plight.

> *These chivalric gentlemen find it quite hard to be confined themselves but do not hesitate to shoot negroes for bringing chickens and berries to sell to the "dammed Yankees," as they call them…My own opinion is they will be fortunate to escape the just retribution of taking up arms against our country. All the Union people I have seen in Virginia say we are too easy with these secessionists and that is my opinion.*

The civilians' petition, however, reached sympathetic ears, as Major General John A. Dix, Wool's successor, ordered the release of those who were not a threat.[121]

The growing number of inmates was an ever-present problem. The following August, disturbed about the difficult summer conditions at the Rip Raps and under pressure from engineers who fretted that they had too little room in which to work, Dix attempted to halt the indiscriminate imprisonment of civilians. His position was grounded partly on political reality. Rebel sympathizers were so numerous that it was impossible to detain "all such persons[;] our forts and prisons would not contain a tithe [tenth] of them." As long as these dissidents went about their business, Dix thought that they should not be bothered. He also felt that "[i]mprisonment at Fort Wool is a most severe punishment at this season. The water is bad and the heat is intense, and no citizen should be sent there for a light cause and without pretty clear evidence of guilt." By August 1863, no prisoners of any kind were found on the Rip Raps.[122]

Chapter 9

THE PRESIDENT IS AT THIS MOMENT AT FORT WOOL

Before the smoke dissipated from the battle of the ironclads, Secretary of War Edwin M. Stanton ordered the name of the citadel on the Rip Raps to be changed. On March 18, 1862, he declared "that in recognition of faithful service by a distinguished and gallant officer, the name of the fort on the Rip Raps is changed from Fort Calhoun to Fort Wool." Stanton thereby elated his fellow members of the radical wing of the Republican Party. He intended to obliterate the name of John C. Calhoun, whom the radicals thought to be the embodiment of the slaveholding South and the secession movement, though when the fort was built its name was thought to honor a "war hawk," a man who stood for American independence in defense of liberty and who opposed European aggression during the War of 1812. Times, positions, and viewpoints had changed drastically.[123]

James Buchanan, the president who preceded Lincoln, was upset over Stanton's decision. Habitually moderate, Buchanan cautioned against the government's action, thinking that it would unnecessarily exasperate and insult Southerners; it would "sink deep into the hearts of the people of the cotton states—men, women, and children." Like many, including Lincoln, Buchanan still thought of Southerners as Americans who would have to be reconciled to the Union after they were defeated. After all, nationalists Henry Clay, Daniel Webster, and others had eulogized John C. Calhoun in death for his elevated character and political contributions. Buchanan noted that Calhoun had passed away before the Compromise of 1850, long before the outbreak of the present rebellion. "Had he been living, I do not think we should be involved in our present difficulties."[124]

Buchanan's moderation was not shared by some Southerners, as the ongoing war shattered lives and disrupted the South. General Ulysses S. Grant's bloody campaign against Richmond and Petersburg and

John E. Wool's fifty-year career ended in 1863 with him serving as the army's fourth ranking general. Carte de visite, Brady's National Portrait Gallery, circa 1863.

General William T. Sherman's destructive march through Georgia and the Carolinas would elicit retorts such as this one from Mary B. Chesnut of South Carolina:

> *At least we will do the North this justice—they do their own thinking. We let one man do ours—Mr. Calhoun. And if fate left us good wine, good dinners, fine horses, and money enough to go abroad every summer, we let things drift, and now we are in this snarl.*[125]

Stanton chose to honor the Rip Raps with the name of one of the longest-serving general officers in the American military, at least up to that time. John Wool, an orphan from Newburgh, New York, had been a book dealer and budding lawyer, but with the onset of the War of 1812 at age twenty-eight he was commissioned a captain in the U.S. Army. Wool performed distinguished and gallant service at the Battles of Queenstown Heights and Plattsburg. In 1816, he was promoted to colonel and appointed inspector general of the army, serving in that capacity until 1841 and justly gaining a reputation as a superb organizer. Wool was in that year appointed brigadier general. During Jackson's administration, he had negotiated the forced removal of the Cherokees to the West, and in the Mexican-American War he had commanded the soldiers that captured Saltillo.

In early May 1862, Abraham Lincoln, Secretary of War Stanton, Treasury Secretary Salmon P. Chase, and Commodore Louis Goldsborough conferred at Fort Monroe to plan the capture of Norfolk and Portsmouth, the home port of the *Virginia*. The president then ventured via tugboat over to Fort Wool, being favorably impressed with its strength, and shared dinner with the garrison. While there he also observed the enemy positions on Sewell's Point and, "watching intently," ordered a shelling of the Rebel battery with the Sawyer Rifle.[126]

Not content to remain at Fort Monroe while his army and navy assailed Sewell's Point and Norfolk, the president and his secretaries boarded a tugboat to cross again to Fort Wool. When the craft made the turn around the island, those aboard saw the wharf with the Sawyer Rifle perched on it. No doubt the eyes of all the soldiers and laborers were on the trio when they stepped onto the timbered landing. It is not known from where the Lincoln party observed the small navy flotilla of wooden steamers that had been assembled for the attack, but it is likely that they either used the dock or watched from atop the upper level of the casemates.

From his Rip Raps vantage point, Salmon Chase described the assault to his daughter, Nettie, as it unfolded:

Abraham Lincoln. Daguerreotype, circa 1863. *Library of Congress.*

Salmon P. Chase. Photograph, Brady's National Portrait Gallery, circa 1860. *Library of Congress*.

It was not a great while before the great ships were in motion. The Seminole *took the lead, the* San Jacinto *and the* Dakota…*and finally the* Susquehanna *followed…with these ships were the* Monitor *and the little gunboat* Stevens…*By and by the* Seminole *reached her position and a belch of smoke, followed in a few seconds by a report like distant thunder, announced the beginning of the cannonade.*

Surely as she read her father's vivid letter Nettie was drawn into the action. "Then came the guns from the Rip Raps where we were and soon the *Monitor* and the *Stevens* joined. In a little while the small battery at the extreme point was silenced, and the cannonade was directed on a battery inside the point a half-mile or a mile nearer Norfolk."[127]

The *New York Herald* reported the effect of Fort Wool's guns:

The very first shell went directly in the rebel camp, its arrival being denoted by a loud report and the rising of a dense column of smoke from the woods in the vicinity…For upward of two hours there were fifty shells thrown at the rebels, with an accuracy of range, aim and effectiveness not to be surpassed. At one time the woods at Sewell's Point were fired at several places, but the wet and sappy nature of the trees prevented its spreading to any great extent.

One of the early shots knocked down the Rebel flagpole.[128]

Stanton telegraphed the War Department that

[t]*he President is at this moment at Fort Wool witnessing our gunboats —three of them besides the Monitor and Stevens—shelling the rebel batteries at Sewell's Point….The Sawyer Gun in Fort Wool has silenced one battery on Sewell's Point. The James rifle mounted on Fort Wool also does good work. It was a beautiful sight to witness the boats moving on to Sewell's Point, and one after another opening fire and blazing away every minute. The troops will be ready in an hour to move…The Merrimac has not made her appearance, but is expected in the field every minute.*[129]

Chase excitedly commented to his daughter: "While this was going on, a smoke curled up over the woods on Sewell's point 5 or 6 miles from its termination, and each man, almost said to the other, 'There comes the *Merrimac*,' and sure enough it was the *Merrimac*."[130]

Virginia was clearly the most dangerous element of the Rebel armament in Hampton Roads, and its appearance changed the entire balance of power.

Virginia steams from Elizabeth River to attack Union ships in line, shelling Sewell's Point. Fort Wool is stylized. Lithograph, 1907. *Naval Historical Center.*

The presidential party prudently returned to Fort Monroe, while the Federal fleet retreated to the shelter of the guns of the two Union forts, ending that day's attack. Chase's judgment of the results of the fight from the Union side was "nobody and nothing hurt," and the intelligence estimate of the remaining strength of the enemy's position supposed that Confederate strength had been damaged, with one battery destroyed. "The [other] results of the rebel side we can't tell but only know that their barracks were burnt by the shells."

From the Confederate perspective, Commodore Josiah Tattnall, commanding the *Virginia*, reported: "I thought [a naval] action certain... [B]efore, however, we got within gunshot of the enemy [they] ceased firing and retired with all speed under the protection of the guns of the fortress, followed by the *Virginia* until the shells from the Rip Raps passed over her."[131]

Lincoln recognized that Sewell's Point could not be reduced by the combined fire from Fort Wool and the Union navy while *Virginia* prowled around Hampton Roads. He decided that the Rebels had to be taken from the rear, with Federal troops disembarking on the farther side of Willoughby

Fort Wool (barely discernible, top) and the *Monitor* (upper right) are near Fort Monroe, as troops embark to invade Norfolk. Watercolor, George Kaiser, 1862. *Mariners' Museum.*

Point, where the *Virginia* could not interfere. As an active commander-in-chief, also not fully trusting his generals and admirals, the president "wished to go and see about it on the spot." He would choose the landing site.

A curious flotilla—with Lincoln and Stanton aboard a tug, "taking with us a large boat and some 20 armed soldiers from the Rip Raps," and with Chase aboard the Treasury Department's *Miami*—navigated that same evening into the Chesapeake Bay and toward the shore along Willoughby Point.[132] Nearing the beach and finding the water too shallow for the tug, the "Rip Raps boat was manned and sent in." At about six o'clock in the evening, Abraham Lincoln stepped onto the sand in Confederate-held territory and found what he judged to be a fine landing spot. The party then immediately departed for the safety of Fort Monroe, where Lincoln "was received with enthusiastic cheering by the troops."

Union shelling from Fort Wool continued to rain down on Sewell's Point throughout the next day as troops assembled at Old Point, boarded their transports, and moved out at midnight, landing the following morning at a stretch of shore actually favored by Chase and Wool. Under General Wool's command, they rapidly took Norfolk, Portsmouth, the Gosport Navy Yard, and the nearby Confederate fortifications. Robert E. Lee, who had supervised the construction of Forts Monroe and Wool and was now commanding the Confederate Army of Northern Virginia, thought that *Virginia* could escape past the forts into the Chesapeake. However, this view was not accepted. With the capture of Gosport, its base, *Virginia* was thought by most to have been rendered ineffective and it was scuttled near Craney Island by the Confederates to keep it out of Union hands.[133]

William F. Keeler aboard the *Monitor* observed "that low dark mass on the water is the Rip Raps, now still and silent, but a few hours since the thunder of its guns bid defiance to rebellion as their flashes lit up the shore." Fort Wool's location and armament thus played a major role in the Federal recapture of the portion of Virginia between Hampton Roads and the Atlantic Ocean,

The Rip Raps, sketched from Fort Monroe. *Harper's Weekly*, June 22, 1861.

opening up the James River as the route to take the Confederate capital at Richmond.[134]

Lincoln thanked the men in the army and navy for this important victory and promoted Wool to major general. On May 11, 1862, Lincoln's order said:

> *The skillful and gallant movements of Maj. Gen. John E. Wool and the forces under his command, which resulted in the surrender of Norfolk and the evacuation of the strong batteries erected by the rebels on Sewell's Point and Craney island and the destruction of the rebel iron-clad steamer Merrimack, are regarded by the President as among the most important successes of the present war.*[135]

"Norfolk is ours: Scene of President Lincoln's first military and naval operation—its success," proclaimed the *New York Herald* on May 12. Wool became a hero in the North. "His achievement in the capture of Norfolk will long be remembered after he shall have departed from life and the scene of strife." However much he praised Wool in public, Lincoln was privately perturbed at the general's indecision once the operation was underway. Lincoln tended to be more of an activist than his generals throughout the war. At this apogee of his military career, Wool was relieved of command and was replaced by General Dix. Although he would enjoy several commands in the quiet northeastern portions of the United States, Wool's active career was over. After fifty-two years of military duty, he retired to New York in 1863, where he resided until his death in 1869, having lived to see restored the Union he served so well and so long.[136]

Similarly, Fort Wool's glory soon faded. After the capitulation of Norfolk and the *Virginia*'s destruction, it was no longer a salient Federal military location. It and Fort Monroe were relegated to serve only as bases of operation for Union land and naval campaigns directed against Confederate Richmond and for quelling widespread dissatisfaction among many Southern sympathizers.

Furthermore, the Federal recapture of Rebel-seized Fort Pulaski near Savannah, Georgia, demonstrated that masonry forts could not withstand the impact of the new rifled artillery, if land-based. A section of the fort was quickly reduced to rubble. Thus were rendered obsolete all of the bastions erected to defend the nation's coast, at great expense and over a long period of time. During the war, such a development could not be acted on, so the seemingly endless drudgery of building dragged along until the Civil War ended.

The termination of hostilities in the Tidewater area was caught by the sharp eye of George Townsend:

> *I studied with intense interest the scene of so many historic events. Sewell's Point lay to the south, a stretch of woody beach, around whose western tip the dreaded* Merrimac *had so often moved slowly to the encounter. The spars of the* Congress *and the* Cumberland *still floated along the strand, but, like them, the invulnerable monster had become the prey of the waves. The guns of the Rip Raps and the terrible broadsides of the*

French watercolorist Prince de Joinville was greatly moved by the sunken *Cumberland* with its masts sadly tilted. *A Civil War Album...,* 1964.

*Federal gunboats, had swept the Confederates from Sewell's Point—their
flag and battery were gone—and farther seaward, at Willoughby Spit,
some figures upon the beach marked the route of the victorious Federals to
the City of Norfolk.* [137]

With Hampton Roads no longer a battlefront, the remaining troops at the
Rip Raps were transferred to Fort Monroe. General Dix wrote in 1863: "To
enable the engineers to go on with the work I have withdrawn the garrison
(181) from Fort Wool." The island was once again the realm of the builder. It
was placed under the superintendence of Major C. Seaforth Stewart of the
Army Engineer Corps with the assistance of a civilian, John Bogart. A large
complement of construction personnel—masons, carpenters, blacksmiths,
and laborers—was employed, and the intensity and scope of the work soon
reached antebellum levels. From June 1863 to June 1864, the stonemasons
and stonecutters prepared and set 800 cubic yards of masonry on the scarp
walls. Laborers continued the grind, removing 3,600 cubic yards of sand
and rocks previously placed to stabilize the substructure. This material by
necessity had blocked some embrasures in the first course of casemates.
Moreover, fifty-two sets of iron rails, the tracks on which the wheeled
seacoast cannon carriages pivoted, were installed in the first-tier casemates.
The expense was not trifling: over $87,200. [138]

Undeniable signs of continued subsidence of the fort's foundation
were discovered. On August 15, 1863, a crack was noticed in the
communication arch of one of the casemates. Soon more fissures were
found in other communication arches. The worst ones were cleaned and
carefully repointed.

Ben Butler, reinstated in command of Hampton Roads, writing to Edwin
Stanton on December 23, 1863, expressed his opinion that, as planned, Fort

John Everding sketched the Rip Raps, showing the second tier of casemates half completed,
rooflines, and cranes with spidery guy wires. *Harper's Weekly*, December 17, 1864.

Wool was obsolete and would never be completed. He understood that the fort's granite walls could not stand the immense weight and power of new armaments. "It would not be finished during your life or mine."

In April 1864, John Hay, secretary to President Lincoln, sailed from Washington to Fort Monroe to meet with Butler. Accompanied by the general, Hay went over to Fort Wool. He saw the Rip Raps as

> *a flattened ellipse—a splendid piece of masonry so far to which two more stories are to be added...The old wall* [the first course of casemates], *whose sinking caused the change and delay in the fort's construction*[,] *is still to be seen, the roughness and imperfect workmanship contrasting sharply with the finish and magnificence of the work of today.*

He also recollected that Butler was "anxious to be allowed to fire at the work from Old Point to test its strength before the building goes any farther." Such experimental shots were apparently never made.[139]

The Rip Raps and other landmarks of the recent battles in Hampton Roads soon became part of the folklore of the rebellion. While future engagements would be waged elsewhere, the memory of the fighting in the area would linger. The epic tale would be told and retold.

The island garrison celebrated Abraham Lincoln's defeat of George B. McClellan, the Democratic candidate, in the critical 1864 presidential election. The harbor was ablaze as all the vessels fired their guns in honor of the president. In late January 1865, the Roads was once again a dramatic but secretive scene of the war. The ill-fated Hampton Roads Peace Conference, between Confederate vice president Alexander H. Stephens and Lincoln, was held aboard a ship anchored near Fort Wool's ramparts.

Fort Wool during the Civil War was both a site of construction and a citadel arrayed for war. For the first and—it turned out—only time in its history engaged in fighting on land and on sea, its significance was threefold. It and Fort Monroe prevented the *Virginia* from breaking out to threaten Washington and sink or disrupt the Federal blockade and shipping. Because of its forward location, the Rip Raps fired far more volleys at the enemy than did Fort Monroe. By supporting the Union fleet during the epic encounter between the *Monitor* and *Virginia* and in the bombardment of Sewell's Point, the fort played an important role in the Union's capture of Norfolk at a time when the Lincoln administration could claim few military successes. While overlooked at the time, removing John C. Calhoun's identity and commemorating General John Wool was an early indication of the vindictive nature of radical Republican prosecution of the remainder of the war and the reconstruction of the South.

Chapter 10

GREAT DERRICKS, LIKE DESERTED GIANTS

After the war, hostility between the North and South did not diminish. Republican president Ulysses S. Grant's administration and Congress imposed a radical reconstruction plan on the vanquished Southern states, which chafed and angered many white Southerners. Economically, times were hard for a region deprived of its workforce and with its chief industry, agriculture, in huge disrepair amid lack of pecuniary resources. Eastern Virginia, in addition, had been scraped and scoured by contending armies. Fort Wool, largely abandoned and deteriorating from neglect, suffered such conflicting passions in the form of vandalism.

The Rip Raps was not garrisoned during Reconstruction, nor was construction continued beyond about 1867. What was accomplished after the war was chiefly limited to building two magazines. Eastern Virginia inhabitants, devastated by the conflict, mostly eked out a sparse existence from farming and timber, also utilizing their small boats to harvest fish and shellfish. Some continued scavenging, a practice that had become commonplace. Fort Wool, with a vast amount of "Yankee" government property, was tempting.

In response to this situation, in 1870 the War Department posted three watchmen on the island who would also conduct minor repairs and painting. Engineer Major William P. Craighill, on July 26, 1872, made a case to General Andrew A. Humphreys, who now commanded the Army Engineers Corps, to extend the tour of duty of such watchmen:

> *Much valuable property* [is] *at Fort Wool, which needs watching night and day being an isolated place and exposed to the pilfering of a class very numerous in that neighborhood who subsist very much in that way and are ready to use violence if necessary to accomplish their object. The isolation*

At the turn of the century, long-disregarded graceful casemates remain, but stone fragments, trees, and underbrush have claimed the parade ground. Photograph, circa 1900.

of Fort Wool and its peculiar exposure to pilfering requires the constant presence of three watchmen.

Craighill was heard, and the detachment was maintained.[140]

During this time of deterioration, many ideas were advanced about what to do with Fort Wool. Jefferson Davis—a former United States secretary of war but who was implicated in the assassination of Lincoln and imprisoned at Fort Monroe from 1865 to 1867—spoke his mind to his captors about the fort once named for his mentor, Calhoun. During a stroll along the south parapet fronting Fort Wool, as he seemed "to prefer this aspect of the compass," he said that since it was nearly completed, it should be fully armed and maintained, as the War Department might find a use for it during a future emergency. However, if the government had it to do over again, it would be wise to use several ironclads, which he knew could defend the roadstead at less than one-tenth the cost.[141]

No plan for the fort's modernization or use existed. On June 30, 1873, Craighill reported that the only work being undertaken at the fort was that "necessary to preserve it from injury," limited to extensive repairs on the wharf and the walkways, which were needed by the watchmen to perform their duties. The next year, Craighill proposed placing several fifteen-inch guns in the barbette there, which could do "good service" in the event of a national emergency. No one now seriously proposed completing the fort, but it seemed practical to mount gun emplacements on the existing works.[142]

Jefferson Davis confined in a casemate at Fort Monroe. Iron bars have been placed in the embrasure. Photograph of sketch, May 29, 1865.

Indeed, the island's chief use in the 1870s and 1880s was other than military. Fort Wool became a place for the advancement of marine science. In the summer of 1878, the secretary of war granted permission to William K. Brooks, a professor of biology at Johns Hopkins University, to establish a Fort Wool research site for his Chesapeake Zoological Laboratory, which conducted an advanced investigation of the bay's fauna. Brooks, colleagues, and students using the existing ramshackle building would work at the island and other sites for ten summer seasons.

Since strong currents ran close to the west end, carrying fifteen or twenty miles of water past the rocks every turn of the tide, multitudes of swimming animals and even embryos were accessible for analysis. The laboratory's significant findings were published in various forms, including standard texts. Several influential papers were published in N.B. Webster's *Partial List of the Land Plants Found at Fort Wool* and P.R. Uhler's *List of Animals Observed at Fort Wool*.

Uhler's work found

> *slight layers of soil upon the surface of large blocks of stone, covering an area of less than six acres, but little can grow to sustain life, and every*

kind of creature found thereon has been brought from some other locality.
Yet, many forms of life are indigenous to the surrounding waters, and a fine
harvest of them may be gathered at most times upon and between the rocks
forming the outer boundary.

Webster discovered more than fifty species of plants growing on the Rip Raps. The "pile of granite rocks, rendered dear to the members of the Chesapeake Bay Zoological Laboratory by their pleasant summer residence there, is interesting, as showing what plants gain a home on almost soilless barren rock and its detritus." It was not probable that any of them had been purposely introduced; rather, their "seeds [were] carried by birds, wafted by winds or water, conveyed in hay, or straw or packing material...or incidentally scattered by soldiers or visitors who threw away peach kernels among the rocks." Any resulting peach trees probably disappeared during a later period of construction at the beginning of the twentieth century.

Brooks and his associates made important contributions concerning the development and habits of the oyster, very important for the Chesapeake's economy, and Brooks published *The Oyster: A Popular Summary of a Scientific Study*. Brooks's was the first marine laboratory in America in which research of purely scientific importance was the ruling feature.[143]

However, the rock pile was indeed a fort, and yet another set of plans to modernize it emanated from the Engineer Corps in 1880. The chief engineer warned Congress that the country's coastal defenses had been neglected, "left to the destructive action of the elements" due to lack of funding. In an emergency they could not be relied on to defend America's important cities and military installations. The technological advances made by powerful European navies posed a threat; now there were "fast war steamers of enormous size, [with] increased iron armor up to two feet in thickness, and rifled guns weighing up to 100 tons carrying a shot of a ton's weight." Devastating attacks might occur surprisingly rapidly. At Fort Wool he recommended substantial modifications that he thought would require several years to achieve: emplacements for and installation of the latest rifled guns, protected by impenetrable iron armor. While it would take an actual threat rather than suppositions and predictions, the report was prescient: such a modernization would be made a quarter century later, immediately after the Spanish-American War.

During this period of zoology and benign neglect, Fort Wool took on a quasi-fantastic aspect. The Rip Raps gradually became shrouded in mystique to the people inhabiting the region and to newcomers. Because of the storied men and events associated with the fort—Robert E. Lee,

Star-Spangled Banner Rising

Fort Wool as viewed from the channel. The rough granite façade had changed little since the Civil War. Photograph, circa 1900.

Andrew Jackson, John Tyler, Abraham Lincoln, the *Virginia* and the *Monitor*, the bombardment of Sewell's Point, and the rest of the Civil War saga—the fortification became romanticized by each side's participants, by writers, and by people near and far. The Victorian era was a time of heightened romanticization anyhow.

Remote and difficult to access, the island stimulated imaginations. Interlopers sneaking onto the island found it eerily frozen in time, with stones, construction debris, and military equipment sprawled about crazily. Simon Bernard's unrealized vision was gradually becoming overgrown from neglect and N.B. Webster's windblown seeds. Visitors cautiously and bravely explored the cavernous and dark casemates and magazines. They probably did not find it difficult to envision the Rip Raps as the setting for a story authored by Edgar Allan Poe or some baroque Victorian novelist.[144]

In fact, one such work was produced. Emma L. Barnes published her novel *Rip Raps* in 1892, exemplifying this common perception. Barnes's romantic murder mystery employed Bernard's two forts as backdrop for the story line. Barnes portrayed young picnickers crossing from Old Point to the Rip Raps, "singing all sorts of songs to the accompaniments of Polly

Young Hampton explorers pose on the rickety wharf about 1893. Remarkably, a pile of loadstones (left) placed before the Civil War remains. Photograph.

The 1893 Hampton Roads Naval Rendezvous honored Christopher Columbus. A colossal statue of Columbus proposed for Fort Wool never materialized. Lithograph. *Library of Congress.*

Dudley's mandolin and Bessie Morton's banjo." Their destination "stands today a grim, grey ruin, a beetle-haunted picnic ground...the landing is so lashed by the conflicting currents that it is always just on the point of tumbling down."

Barnes had obviously visited the Rip Raps. Her fictive young people walked

over the sharp stones, through a dense growth of fragrant may-weed, they wended their way until they finally reached the broad paved casemates. Great derricks, like deserted giants, lay prone; huge chains huddled together in a rusty mass, while broken gun-swivels, spikes and other enginery of war attested their wasted lives.

Polly Dudley was impatient to "explore every nook and cranny of the subterranean vault or magazine into which daylight never penetrated and she expressed her determination to plunge into its mysterious depths." Barnes's disheveled romantic Victorian retreat was, in 1900, much closer to the reality of Fort Wool than any military use.

Chapter 11

DISAPPEARING GUNS

Anew era in the construction of American coastal defenses was ushered in by the plans of the Endicott Board. Chaired by President Cleveland's secretary of war, William C. Endicott, the board in 1886 proposed significantly modernizing the woefully antiquated battlements along all coasts. Masonry would not give protection against the projectiles of modern naval weaponry. Cement, steel, and concrete were necessary. Huge rifled artillery pieces with firing ranges measured in miles were also demanded for the nation's security.[145]

With building materials collected previously, construction began on the new concept for Fort Wool in 1902. The Endicott fortification would display a strikingly different style of architecture from the previous mass of granite and brick held together by mortar and iron pinions. The nineteenth-century fort was intended to reach a height of four tiers and to be equipped with a multitude of guns, concentrating firepower vertically because of the island's small size and incidentally overawing any enemy who could see it. The newer steel and concrete batteries would be more streamlined at only one tier in elevation, incorporating many fewer but infinitely more powerful guns, and could be manned by a significantly smaller number of artillerymen. It was designed to strike much more distant targets, so the troops would have to be better trained in technology and firing methodology.

The Rip Raps was once again a hectic construction site. The daunting undertaking of dismantling and removing the archaic granite walls and casemates was begun. Eight casemates situated on the west end of the island were left undisturbed. The lower section of the gorge wall was left intact, while the upper portion of the wall and the rest of the casemates of the original work were demolished. Stiff-leg derricks dismantled the fort stone by stone. A locomotive and a railroad track were employed to move the

The Jacksonian-era fort with its castlelike appearance, before being dismantled. Souvenir album, circa 1895.

stone. Apparently, some of the material was incorporated as fill in the new structure, while other pieces were hauled away. Because the new fort was erected atop the remnants of the earlier structure, it followed the trace and retained the basic shape of the earlier fort. In places, granite block outlines can still be seen beneath a veneer of Endicott cement.

Rebuilding began on the west end in June 1902 on two three-inch rapid-fire gun batteries, sandwiching the remnants of the old stone fort. The first, fronting the gorge, was finished on May 25, 1905, soon followed by the second battery, fronting the bay, completed on September 30, 1905. These guns were designed to protect a minefield placed in the deep channel and to guard against small boat attack. Three disappearing gun batteries were then begun, each mounting two six-inch M1903 guns on M1903 disappearing carriages. The first was next to the bay-side rapid-fire battery, followed by a second, moving eastward along the bay side of the island, and the third was at the island's east end. Work on the batteries commenced on December 10, 1903, and finished in August 1908. The four bay-side emplacements filled almost all of the space that had originally been occupied by the antebellum casemates.[146]

Contractors from Virginia, Maryland, Pennsylvania, and New York submitted bids to the chief engineer's office at the customhouse in Norfolk for the materials that the government specified for the project. Yellow pine was delivered for fashioning forms to hold the innumerable yards of concrete. In 1904 alone, aside from sand, 14,200 barrels of Portland cement and 7,900

Gun well for disappearing gun at Fort Wool, as it appears today. Photograph, 2009. *David K. Hazzard.*

Complementing Fort Wool's armament, ten- and twelve-inch disappearing guns (such as this one, with its large crew) were installed at Fort Monroe. Photograph, circa 1917. *City of Hampton.*

cubic yards of broken stone used as aggregate in the mix were delivered to the island.[147]

A concrete mixing plant was set up, and runways were laid for the men to move materials to construction areas. Pouring and finishing the concrete for the massive batteries was hard and unforgiving work. Scores of men were required, and they were eager to work, as times were once again hard in America. The steamship *Phillips* ferried workers back and forth and carried supplies and water to the fort. Carpenters and their helpers performed the repetitive job of nailing wooden forms together. In the heat of Virginia's oppressive summer days, laborers sweated profusely to pour yard after yard of concrete into the forms. Finishers shaped the surfaces.

On December 27, 1904, the War Department gave official names to the Fort Wool batteries in order to recognize the contributions of noteworthy soldiers in past wars. The gorge-side rapid-fire gun battery was named for Robert E. Lee's father, Henry "Light Horse Harry" Lee, a cavalry general in the Continental army during the American Revolution. The bay-side rapid-fire battery honored Jacob Hindman, one of the most respected artillerists in the War of 1812. Next to it, Battery Claiborne, a disappearing gun battery, was named in remembrance of Ferdinand L. Claiborne, who fought the Creek Indians in Alabama and served in the War of 1812. The middle disappearing gun battery was dedicated to Alexander B. Dyer, the army's chief of ordnance at the end of the Civil War. The easternmost disappearing gun battery carried the name of Horatio Gates, who was credited with the pivotal victory at the Battle of Saratoga during America's War for Independence.[148]

Battery Gates was of critical importance, fronting the Chesapeake Bay whence an enemy would come and coincidentally on the site of Andrew Jackson's secluded hut. Fort Wool's six disappearing guns, mounted on Buffington-Crozier carriages, had ranges of about six miles. Their twenty-six-foot, five-inch barrels were made at the Watervliet Arsenal. The disappearing carriages, produced at the Detrick and Harvey Machine Company, had been perfected by Americans Adelbert R. Buffington and William Crozier.[149]

These guns were recessed in pits open to the sky but below ten-foot walls and thus not normally visible from the sea. Raised up for firing when the men released a counterweight suspended below the carriage, each gun moved to the rear and downward with the recoil of a shot, once again out of sight from the water. In the lowered position and secure behind the concrete wall, a gun was reloaded from the breech. From the magazines the gun crews delivered shells and powder charges on wheeled shot carts. Located near the guns, each battery had a coincidence range finder. Inside the walls of the batteries were plotting rooms and artillery shell rooms. A proficient crew could fire a gun twice in sixty seconds. Several years later, battery commander stations were added to coordinate firing information.

Battery Lee mounted four rapid-fire guns, while its companion, Battery Hindman, boasted two. The guns were fixed in horseshoe-shaped pits with low parapets. Each gun had a thick shield for protection. Shells were taken from magazines situated within the batteries and passed by hand up to the waiting crew. Between these two batteries the lone remaining section of casemates stood as a reminder of the failure, after untold expense and time, of the early engineers to complete the work. Conversely, it formed a monument to the master workmanship and design of a bygone era. The Endicott-era engineers had the satisfaction of actually finishing their fort's design and mounting all of its guns—the first and only time in the storied history of Fort Wool that such was true.

The Jamestown Exposition of 1907 commemorated America's 300th anniversary. Held at Sewell's Point near the Confederate fortification from forty-five years earlier, it celebrated the nation's history with particular emphasis on advances in technology. Americans were flush with victory over a European power in the Spanish-American War and were supremely confident in their future. Business was booming as J.P. Morgan, John D. Rockefeller, Andrew Carnegie, and other entrepreneurs developed massive steel, railroad, and other industries. Thousands of visitors toured the exposition and partook of excursions to nearby Jamestown and other historic sites. Forts Monroe and Wool proved to be immensely popular.

One exposition guidebook gloried in Fort Wool's history, noting that "[d]uring the Civil War the garrison [participated]…in the famous battle of the *Monitor* and *Merrimac*." It also stressed recent advancements in weaponry. The fort "is equipped with immense disappearing guns and the latest machinery for defense in time of war. With Fortress Monroe and the Rip Raps, Tidewater Virginia is amply protected from the assault of any possible enemy by water."[150]

America's prosperity and expansion of empire was manifested in the development of a new steel navy. On December 16, 1907, President Theodore Roosevelt boastfully dispatched a flotilla of sixteen battleships, dubbed "the Great White Fleet," from Hampton Roads on an around-the-world cruise. The demonstration was meant to impress on Japan and other nations that with such naval might backed up by such industrial production the United States was seizing a well-deserved front-row seat in the order of nations. Two years later, the fleet returned to a grand salute viewed by the triumphant president, nearing the end of his second term in office. Fort

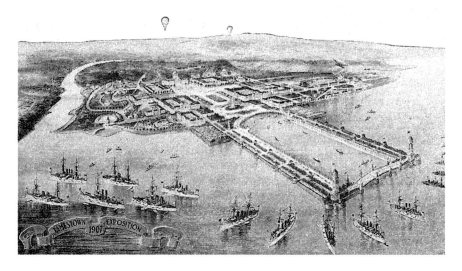

A miniature city was built for the 1907 Jamestown Exposition, with buildings for governments, manufacturers, and organizations worldwide. Postcard. *Jerry & Bonnie Karwac.*

This Jamestown Exposition postcard contrasts the old fort's stone casemate remnants (right) with recently completed concrete Endicott fortifications (left). 1907.

Star-Spangled Banner Rising

Ships of the Great White Fleet, preparing for their two-year worldwide cruise, viewed from the Chamberlin Hotel at Old Point Comfort. Promotional image, 1907. *U.S. Naval Historical Center.*

Wool, with its shining steel disappearing guns arrayed on the new streamlined concrete citadel, provided a fitting backdrop when Roosevelt's great array of gleaming white ships steamed by.

However, surprisingly enough, no one was home. As the War Department's 1908 annual report stated, several posts, including Fort Wool, "have been authorized [their complement of men] but not yet garrisoned." Troops would not be stationed there until after a barracks and other buildings were finished. During this era, Fort Wool's parade ground was torn up and disorderly, as it had been in much of the past. The years of construction crews endeavoring to erect the fort, its varying gun emplacements, and a series of temporary buildings had taken their toll. Makeshift walkways and pieces of building material littered the place.

Extraordinarily, the barracks for the caretaker crew completed in November 1910 was the only major structure built during the long course of Fort Wool's history actually intended to stand for many years. Its architectural style blended in well with the Endicott generation of defenses. The single-story barracks was made of substantial materials, with walls of brick and a slate roof. Electricity, becoming common throughout America, illuminated the interior. Heat was provided by stoves. Enlisted men with their personal gear were to bunk in a dormitory, which was furnished with ten iron-frame bunks and as many wall lockers, while one noncommissioned officer would be quartered in a bay adjacent to his charges. Soldiers were to take their daily meals in the mess, which had a kitchen, a refrigerator, and a handy pantry. Clothing was cleaned in the laundry's two large washtubs. The latrine consisted of a shower and only a single toilet and urinal.[151]

The utilitarian sewage water supply for Fort Wool was stored inside a 3,500-gallon tank, which since 1896 had provided saltwater flushing for Fort

Brick barracks nearing completion. Photograph, 1910. *United States War Department.*

Monroe's sewage system. In 1910, it was relocated to the Rip Raps. The tank, ten feet high and eight feet in diameter, sat on top of a brick foundation, with a galvanized interior and a wooden roof. A storage building made of sheet iron with a concrete floor was ready for use in 1910.[152]

In May 1916, a new fire control station was added to the island's defenses. The two-story wooden building with a tin roof was placed at the foot of the wharf landing. It was designed to enclose a fifteen-foot range finder mounted on a solid concrete column as tall as the station. A winding exterior stairway led to the roof, which was flat with a railing. It rose about twelve feet above the east and northeast batteries, which would shield it to some extent from enemy fire.[153]

At the same time, a concrete cable hut was finished, sited on the island's edge near the wharf. From here, underwater communication cables were run to Fort Monroe.

Fort Wool's place in the region's security was heightened when the United States entered the First World War in April 1917, and other vital military installations were created in the Hampton Roads vicinity. A huge Naval Operating Base was established on nearly five hundred acres of

Water tower rises from a parade ground barren of grass and cluttered with cable spools, barrels, and buildings. Photograph, 1910. *United States War Department.*

Now mostly Endicott concrete, Fort Wool is starkly silhouetted against a backdrop of sparsely built-up Willoughby Point. Postcard, circa 1917.

Eighth Company Guardsmen, facing a frigid winter quartered in tents while the barracks are under construction, assemble in front of Battery Claiborne. Detail, photograph, 1917.

land at Sewell's Point. Construction crews built piers, storehouses, railroad connections, and facilities for fuel and oil storage. Dredging in Hampton Roads opened the way for large ships and submarines to dock. By war's end, thirty-four thousand men were stationed there. The military had also, somewhat suddenly, ascended into the heavens. A naval air station, located adjacent to the naval base, was also built, while about the same time the Army Air Corps founded its first base, Langley Field, in cow pastures on Back River near Hampton. Pilots flying above Fort Wool aimed their cameras while training in aerial photography.

The island was manned during the First World War by the Eighth Company, Virginia Coast Artillery, National Guard. Under the command of Captain Beverly D. Harwood, they were mainly a group of volunteers from Virginia's nearby, rural Gloucester and Mathews Counties. Many of the men were farmers and watermen, at home in the Fort Wool environment. Ordered to Fort Monroe in August 1917 and soon transferred to the Rip

Raps, they endured a harsh winter, as recounted by Gloucester resident Mary W. Gray:

> *How these poor fellows suffered in the winter that followed, for it was one of the coldest that Virginia has ever had. The poor soldiers on Fort Wool, with the waters of Hampton Roads frozen in a wall around them, some times almost froze. There were so many soldiers to be outfitted in the United States that year that many of them had insufficient clothing and other covers.*[154]

The parade ground took on a new configuration of temporary structures to accommodate a garrison much larger than anticipated by the earlier construction. These included army-issued tents at first, then one large and two smaller barracks, a mess hall, a common bathhouse, and a coal shed. Coal was used to stoke potbellied stoves. A new wharf was now situated to the east of the jetty of stone that had supported the original nineteenth-century landing place, fronting the administration building. Battered by the ceaseless waves and often harsh weather of Hampton Roads, wharves at the Rip Raps always had short lives.[155]

Despite the larger complement of men, Fort Wool's armament was significantly reduced because of the severity of need that emerged during the war. In accordance with a directive of July 18, 1918, the firing tubes of the four disappearing guns of Batteries Gates and Dyer disappeared, being transported to Europe. Battery Claiborne's remaining two gun barrels were dislodged from their carriages and remounted on the empty carriages at Gates, fronting the open sea. Claiborne's carriages were to be scrapped. All of the three-inch guns remained.

World War I ended in November 1918, and once again Fort Wool moved to caretaker status. The troops dispersed, and only a small contingent of men was stationed there. The men performed maintenance duties such as looking after the island's power plant and caring for the guns, primarily to prevent rusting. Minor additions to the fort continued sporadically. In early December 1921, for example, a new station for the coincidence range finder was placed in service. It was located on Battery Dyer's parapet between the gun emplacements.[156]

The fort's cavernous magazines were used to stockpile hazardous ammunition and mine equipment for use at Forts Monroe and Story (located at Cape Henry) when needed. As had happened before, the wharf deteriorated and was close to collapse when, in September 1932, emergency funding was requested to rebuild it. A new wharf, 104 feet long by 14 feet wide, opened in late June 1933.

Young Elizabeth Newton, daughter of Fort Wool's caretakers, pulls her wagon in front of barracks, oblivious to the Great Depression. Photograph, 1933.

At the same time, improvements to the nearby lighthouse station at Old Point Comfort were made. In 1936, an experimental apparatus was added to control the fog signal for Hampton Roads. A light beam was sent in two-minute intervals from Fort Wool and received by a photoelectric cell at Old Point. If the cell did not pick up the light beam, this meant that it had been impeded by fog, rain, or snow, and the fog signal was activated.

In the midst of the Great Depression, civilian caretaker Charles V. Newton, his wife Elizabeth, and their young daughter resided on the island. Government vessels brought water and other necessities to them. To their daughter the fort was a playground, where everything was possible. The island had a series of caretakers like the Newtons, whose children, living an isolated life, were shy because they were not accustomed to strangers.[157]

Even during the Depression, the waters surrounding the Rip Raps were filled with craft. Picturesque Old Bay Line steamships churned by as they provided a major mode of transportation for people and goods, mostly seafood, between Norfolk, Old Point, Washington, and Baltimore. Black and

Star-Spangled Banner Rising

Old Bay Line steamship leaving Old Point Comfort for Baltimore, about to pass Fort Wool. Postcard, circa 1940.

white men aboard sleek log canoes—some under sail, some now fitted with engines—made a slim living on the water harvesting oysters and fish. Large buy boats weighed down with oysters passed on their way to packing plants in Hampton and Norfolk. Other watermen in smaller crab boats made their catches. For these mariners, the heap of rocks was an accustomed sight that their forefathers had known well, part of the folklore of the water.

Chapter 12

NOTHING BUT ROCKS
TO THROW AT THE INVADER

I mmediately prior to the Second World War, with the prospect of a major
naval threat from the Axis powers, the existing armament of American
harbor defenses seemed ill-equipped to perform their missions. Additional
long-range guns were desirable for the perimeter forts of Chesapeake Bay.
A total reassessment of the nation's harbor defense system was performed.
In July 1940, the Harbor Defense Board proposed the construction of new
batteries at various bay fortifications, with guns providing firepower with
ranges up to twenty-five miles. Included would be a new six-inch, two-gun
battery at Fort Wool with a maximum range of approximately fifteen miles,
effective against light cruisers and other smaller vessels.[158]

With the advent of war in December 1941, the defense of the lower
Chesapeake Bay was shared among Fort Story at Cape Henry and Fort John
Custis on Cape Charles, bracketing the bay's twelve-mile-wide entrance,
and Forts Wool and Monroe, holding responsibility for Hampton Roads,
as well as for the bay's waters between Buckroe and Ocean View. Wartime
traffic was heavy. At the conflict's height, an average of eighty-seven ships a
day entered the bay.

A minefield was laid in the waters near Thimble Shoals, and an
antisubmarine net was stretched between the two forts, where the original
plans had called for a boom raft. The mines were distributed by a "mine-
planter," the *J.M. Schofield*, which docked at Fort Monroe. Early on, tugboats
were used to pull the submarine net out to block the channel, but thereafter
specially built vessels with cranes were used to position the net.[159]

At one point, Alec Guinness, the noted actor serving as a British naval
captain, ran afoul of the antisubmarine net. Guinness remembered:

Night had fallen, weather conditions were appalling, there were no navigational aids (I could spread out the excuses) and I managed to get one third of my ship straddled across the [net] designed, so they thought, to stop penetration by the enemy. We struggled off our spider's web in an hour or so... Visibility was nil, so, having backed away from the [net], I dropped anchor. The first light of day was an alarming revelation; together with half a dozen other LCIs we had anchored in the middle of a mine field. The tide had gone down and the mines could be seen a foot below the surface, slowly swaying like sinister black balloons.

Guinness and his ship thankfully survived.[160]

Following the surprise Japanese attack at Pearl Harbor, all American military units went on alert. The Virginia Peninsula—an extremely important defense center because it contained the army's Langley Field, Fort Monroe, Fort Wool, and Fort Eustis, plus the massive Newport News Shipbuilding and Dry Dock Co. and the naval mine depot at Yorktown—saw these military units hurriedly put in readiness for all possible eventualities. Urgency demanded that the orders of commanding officers be relayed to their men through civilian radio stations.

When the news first flashed of the attack on Honolulu, local soldiers could hardly restrain their enthusiasm after years of tense standoffs, marking time while Europe became engulfed in war. Furloughs and leaves of absence were cancelled. Ferry, bus, and railway stations were centers of activity as men in uniform answered the call to hurry to their commands, having taken leave of family and friends in response to the new emergency. Lights at Fort Monroe's headquarters of the Harbor Defense of Chesapeake Bay burned all night.[161]

Carrying only a few items of personal gear, the men of Battery D of the Second Coast Artillery were mobilized, loaded onto boats, and sent to Fort Wool. This happened so hastily that Lieutenant M.G. Stroud recalled, "There was no armament, no ammunition, no food, no nothing! We sat around all night with nothing but rocks to throw at the invader."[162]

Fort Wool was "so near and yet so far" from the mainland. All food, water, coal, and supplies had to be transported by boat to the fort. Once during a shortage, the men had to drink water gathered from the roofs of buildings. Enlisted man Horace L. Gifford, who was stationed there for three years, remembered that "living on that island was no bed of roses." The men spent the first winter bunked in tents, up to fifty men per shelter. One night, a northeaster blew down most of the tents, and the remainder of that frigid evening was endured in one of the magazines. A welcomed seasonal respite for the beleaguered men arrived on December 25 in the guise of Christmas dinner, with a menu of roast turkey, mashed potatoes, cranberry sauce, and mince pie.[163]

Owing to high water and sometimes unforgiving winds, the island had little or no dirt, being mostly a rocky surface when the soldiers arrived. Sergeant Charles McIntyre dispatched successive details of men to the mainland to gather dirt in the area of Big Bethel, the scene of a Civil War battle. Sacks of rich soil were trucked to the wharf at Old Point Comfort, transported to the island by tugboat, and distributed over the parade ground to be planted in grass. McIntyre was the "fellow who built the sidewalks" to make it easier to traverse the island.[164]

Goats kept the grass trimmed in military fashion but at little cost. The agile animals were ideal for negotiating the sloped, grassy berms atop the magazines. They became mascots to the men, who cared for them and found them playful, enjoyable companions. Gifford recalled, "It was lonesome on Fort Wool…we had two billy goats to amuse us during my stay on the island."[165]

Another pet was Lady, a gentle German shepherd, who became a familiar sight. Belonging to one of the troops from Gloucester County, she had a litter of puppies on the fateful evening of December 7. A photograph of Lady and her puppies found its way into the local newspaper alongside all the dire events of the rapidly developing war. The dogs enjoyed the run of the place and were quickly befriended by the soldiers. When Lady died in October 1945, she was buried outside one of the barracks, and a stone was inscribed with her name.

With Americans now concerned about Japanese attacks by air, machine guns protected by sandbags were hastily positioned on Batteries Claiborne and Dyer. These makeshift defenses were replaced on October 22, 1942, when two fifty-caliber antiaircraft machine guns were placed at Batteries Hindman and Gates. They were protected by substantial concrete walls. Sabotage, especially early on, was a concern for the small garrison. Barbed wire was strung from iron rods shaped like giant corkscrews placed around the island's edges. Guards in battle gear walked the perimeter.

In the cold winter of 1942, several temporary buildings were thrown up by civilian contractors traveling over to the island daily. Six barracks were erected to house about thirty men each, framed with two-by-fours covered by plywood and sheathed with tar paper held in place with furring strips. A series of windows provided ventilation. With a potbellied stove in each, rows of metal-framed cots, foot lockers, and wall lockers filled the rooms. Winds would whistle up through the floorboards. The once again crowded parade

On high alert at the outset of war, a sentry armed with fixed bayonet and ammunition belt stands atop the old fort. Photograph, 1941.

Star-Spangled Banner Rising

Soldiers at the ready at the old casemate citadel. This image was taken two weeks after the attack on Pearl Harbor. Photograph, 1941.

Structures clutter the parade ground—barracks (foreground), latrine (center), and water tower—while a sandbagged machine gun nest sits atop the rampart (left). Photograph, 1942.

With civilian life behind, men pass time in crowded, stark barracks amid military cots, wall lockers and foot lockers, and a potbellied stove. Photograph, circa 1942.

Christmas dinner with turkey and apples awaits the troops in the mess hall adorned with individual menus, ribbons, and tinsel hung from ceiling. Photograph, circa 1942.

ground also contained an officers' quarters, a recreation building, a latrine, a supply building, and a mess hall.

Although the buildings served the men for the duration of the war, Fort Wool was restructured with up-to-date technology and defenses. A newly erected battery commander station was ready for action in late October 1942. Its design was striking—a double-story reinforced concrete superstructure with a wooden roof atop a thirty-six-foot steel tower. The station's second level was cantilevered precariously over the first section and had narrow observation openings on three sides of the boxlike structure. From within the station, officers would coordinate with other batteries defending Hampton Roads by means of telephones and would direct the installation's artillery fire. To protect personnel from the cold, heaters were installed, along with a small latrine so they would not have to leave in time of emergency.[166]

The azimuth instrument and the coincidence range finder, the observing instruments, were housed in this building. Even in wartime, pleasure boats cruised the waterways on summer days, and Corporal Thomas Fazenbacker used the fort's range finders to watch young ladies sunning themselves aboard nearby boats.[167]

The construction of Battery 229 marked the third and last type of fortification to be placed on the venerable Rip Raps. Its installation was pursuant to the July 1940 report of the Harbor Defense Board. Positioned on the island's eastern tip, its two guns were to be embedded on top of a massive bunker made of reinforced concrete and structural steel. The old guns were removed, and the larger part of Battery Gates was demolished to make way for the new facility.

Crews began the project on March 31, 1943. Concrete with stone aggregate poured forth daily from a bulky mixer. Carpenters nailed together wooden forms to hold into place yard after yard of concrete. The battery emplacement was completed on January 31, 1944, but the weapons were never finished. The carriages and shields were installed, but the gun tubes were not.

Battery 229 was secure and self-contained, meaning that with the fear of gas attacks the facility could be tightly closed up, and there were specially designed doors and exhaust closures. Its interior was a maze of corridors leading to rooms designated for battery fire control, ammunition, power, and storage. The remaining Endicott-era terra-cotta tiles and concrete walls were incorporated into the new construction.

There were three shell rooms. Powder and an arsenal of charges were stored in two dry rooms protected with iron doors. A dehumidifying unit, a Carrier "Weathermaker," ventilated the whole battery complex. Forced

The roof is now missing from the battery commander station, but it is the tallest structure remaining on the island. Photograph, 2009. *David K. Hazzard.*

Standing in front of the 1910 building in combat gear, Corporal Thomas
Fazenbaker of Westernport, Maryland, brandishes a 1903 Springfield rifle.
Photograph, 1942.

In winter 1942, a gun crew and the remaining garrison assemble beside a disappearing gun at Battery Gates. Sentries stand vigilant near a guardhouse. Photograph.

FORT WOOL

A rare interior view showing magazines with stacks of artillery shells inside Battery Gates. Troops obeyed the "no smoking" sign, no doubt. Photograph, circa 1945.

Fort Wool as it looks today. World War II remnants include Battery 229 at left end and battery commander station, left center. Photograph, Joe Fudge, 2000.

hot water pipes heated the power and water cooler rooms, while electric dehumidifying units heated the battery's nerve center with its plotting board, the spotting room, and the latrine. The power room contained three diesel electric generators.

Artillery fire would be directed by model 296 radar, recently developed at the Massachusetts Institute of Technology. Once a waterborne target was observed, the device would precisely determine the range and azimuth to the ship. Completed in September 1943, the steel radar tower was more than one hundred feet high—the tallest structure ever built at Fort Wool—and was erected on a substantial concrete foundation at the west end of the island, just outside the remnants of the original fort. It was unfortunately dismantled at the war's end.

Its mechanical components were placed inside a newly built room composed of hollow tiles, built within the nineteenth-century casemates. A sheet of concrete covered most of the old stone flooring. Complex electronic transmitting and generating equipment included the radar set, mounted in a large cabinet. The space was illuminated by incandescent light, while an oil burner offered heat and twin Leroi motor generators set on concrete pedestals provided power. Several men were required to operate the station.[168]

Radar tower on island's western tip looms over old casemate remnants. Next to it is a searchlight tower. Photograph, circa 1945.

In a vivid picture of gun crew action, GIs passing shells from man to man load breech of a Battery Hindman rapid-fire gun. Photograph, 1942.

On August 2, 1943, yet another addition to the developing defenses was ready for use: the battery commander and coincidence range finder station. Located above the radar room, on the second level of the old nineteenth-century stone fort, it was a curious blending of the past and present. A concrete slab, eight inches in thickness, was poured on the earlier surface of stone, forming the station's base. Its basic, boxlike, reinforced concrete double-tier design contrasted sharply with the surrounding granite stonework. The station enclosed an azimuth instrument and a range finder supporting the still-in-place rapid-fire guns of Battery Hindman when in action.[169]

Searchlights had been installed in the 1920s and were replaced in the 1930s. They rested on platforms atop two towers, one at each end of the island, on iron tracks secured to concrete floors. The lighting apparatus was housed behind large removable tin shutters and was operated from the coincidence range finder station atop Battery Dyer. The lights illuminated the busy channel, allowing personnel to monitor the harbor's traffic at night.

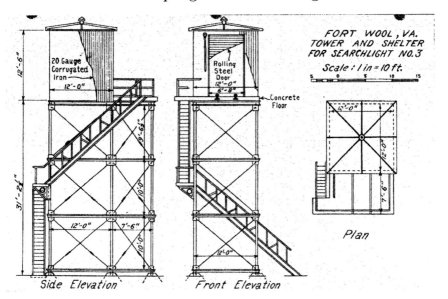

Engineer's drawing for the two searchlight towers. They replaced older wooden towers that were converted into navigation lights. Plan, 1930. *United States War Department.*

With 160 enlisted men and 6 officers garrisoned at the fort, and with the parade ground, as usual, filled with utilitarian structures, "Top" Sergeant McIntyre recalled that the lack of individual space often caused tempers to flare. Forced to drill the men in this restricted space, McIntyre frequently resorted to marching them out onto the wharf and back. Despite these disadvantages, they achieved honors in Fort Monroe reviews.[170]

A store or "PX" (Post Exchange) was established in one of the magazines within Battery Lee, operated for a time by garrison member Corporal Randolph Bender. Orders were taken from the troops, and goods were purchased and brought over from Fort Monroe. Makeshift shelves were lined with items such as cigarettes, candy, razor blades, and chewing gum.[171]

Coca-Cola consumption was a popular leisure time activity on the Rip Raps, and a vending machine was installed to dispense sodas to thirsty troops. Company executive Robert Woodruff vowed that he wanted to "see that every man in uniform gets a bottle of Coca-Cola for 5 cents wherever he is and whatever the cost to the company." At the end of the war, it was estimated that five billion bottles of the popular soft drink had been consumed worldwide. Soda bottle fragments are the most common artifact found on the island.

Dances were held on the island to break the soldiers' dreary routine. Local young women arrived by boat in the evening and were escorted to the

First Sergeant Charles McIntyre (left), of Philadelphia, a soldier's soldier who took care of his men, poses with Staff Sergeant Downie Wray. Photograph, circa 1942.

Smiling soldier holds a Coca-Cola bottle as an eager billy goat consumes the classic American beverage. Photograph, circa 1943.

Men kneel during a religious service in one of the Endicott-era magazines. Ammunition boxes support the makeshift altar. Photograph, circa 1943.

Christmas dinner guests are Mrs. Walter Scott, Marysville, Kansas; Fay Martin, San Antonio; Mrs. Vincent D'Amico, Bridgeport, Connecticut; and Mrs. Charles McIntyre, Norfolk. Photograph, 1942.

building where the "shindig" was to take place. They saw nothing of the rest of the island, remembering only that it was very dark. There are stories that comedian Red Skelton came to the Rip Raps to entertain the troops and that he got seasick on the boat trip over.

Walter Winchell, probably the most popular radio broadcaster of the time, reported on a Sunday evening to the nation that Fort Monroe was full of able men who could be sent to the war zones. In what seems apocryphal, one amazed veteran remembered that in less than a week, about half of the troops were moving out, including many of those at Fort Wool.[172]

When hostilities ceased, all remaining troops at Fort Wool departed. The installation would never again house armed military personnel or be used for military purposes, and it began to fall into neglect.

Chapter 13

DEADER THAN
FOUR O'CLOCK

In the immediate postwar era, Corporal Leon Hales headed a seven-member resident army crew charged with maintaining the island. Their duties included inspecting the diesel engines and making general repairs. Their time was not unpleasant, as duties were not onerous. They had plenty of shore passes, and the boat to Fort Monroe ran on a regular basis. Playing cards, especially gin rummy, helped to pass the time. Pets included several goats—one named Satan and one ironically called Billy—a few dogs and a cat, all of which helped break the monotony.[173]

Soon the Fort Wool crew diminished. From January 1947 to May 1948, Sergeant Ray C. Alexander was assigned as sole caretaker. He lived on the island with Virginia, his wife, and their young son, Michael, who played amongst the empty concrete emplacements with his toy scooter while their dog Razz and cat Tom romped with him. Ray maintained the island well until the army decided to discontinue resident caretakers, and he was transferred to Fort Story. These people thought of the Rip Raps as home, and the memory of life on the island was part of the family legacy even after the passing of many years.[174]

The decreasing level of army interest demonstrated that the Rip Raps had outlived its military usefulness. After May 1948, with a caretaker sergeant visiting only two or three times a week, Fort Wool became overgrown with weeds, trees, and shrubs. The *Norfolk Ledger-Dispatch* on October 27, 1949, portrayed the state of Fort Wool in the following way: "Waves break on the sharp rocks…There are no guns on the fort, no electric lights and no drinking water, but the telephone works. The rocky shores are covered with flotsam and weeds grow high in the little bit of dirt…Fort Wool is deader than four o'clock." The dogs and cats that once prowled were gone, and now there were "lots of rats." Rodents became the denizens of Fort Wool.

Caretaker Ray Alexander and wife, Virginia, visit Fort Wool after a fifty-year absence "to see the old fort at least one more time." Photograph, 1990.

Old-timers return again and again to the stone island of their youth and their home during the war. Here Horace Gifford reminisces with guide Chris Bennett. Photograph, 1991.

Now barracks and latrine, declared obsolete, are gone. The lofty radar tower still stands but will be disposed of in the coming winter. Photograph, 1945.

Deterioration plagued the few remaining casemates with their splendid granite and brick work. The infamous cracks in the brick barrel-vaulted ceilings and even in the stone walls, piers, and arches first seen so long ago continued to open and lengthen as water passed through, washing out the mortar. Rainwater dripped from the ceilings, and the interiors were damp. As the mass of the structure continued to settle, the scarp wall was pushed farther outward. The Totten iron embrasures weathered. The Endicott and Second World War concrete cracked and spalled.

Fort Wool in the 1950s remained in abandonment both an imposing reminder of bygone days and an eerie mass of rock difficult to reach by boat. Firing from the disappearing guns that once rattled the windows of buildings in the nearby town of Phoebus had ceased for good. And the traces of the artillerymen who once inhabited the island had all but vanished. Myths grew up with the weeds, such as the widely held notion that the fort had been constructed from ballast stone pitched overboard by the crews of colonial-era vessels.

Symbolizing the state of Fort Wool's decline was the wooden sign designating it as a Harbor Defense Command during World War II lying upended on the ground. Driftwood and debris of all descriptions collected along the rocky shore. As after previous wars, salvagers stripped the place of metal objects; a generator, for example, found its way to a Virginia Beach service station.

Fort Wool was a post in the Harbor Defense of Chesapeake Bay system during (and after) World War II. Photograph, 1947.

A rash visitor would encounter a foreboding sign mounted on the wharf stating "No Trespassing U.S. Government Property Violators Will Be Prosecuted." Nevertheless, over the years adventuresome boaters explored the Rip Raps. The Battery Control Tower, the site's most prominent remaining feature, offered a magnificent panoramic view after one made the precarious climb up rusted-out steps, watching carefully for the several places lacking guardrails. The massive concrete gun wells that once mounted artillery had become ghostlike, and entry doors marked "Powder Room" and "3-Inch Ammunition" served as reminders of the island's former use.[175]

In the 1950s, the Hampton Roads Bridge-Tunnel was built to connect Norfolk with the peninsula, and the southern tunnel entrance was located on a new man-made island adjacent to Fort Wool. Ironically, engineers encountered many of the same vexing difficulties that the army had faced over a century before. Test borings confirmed that there was a soft sandy bottom at least eighty feet deep.[176]

The building techniques used in forming the south island were similar to those used when constructing the Rip Raps. Barges loaded with large granite boulders were moored over the site. Each boulder was hoisted by

Fort Wool, a National Historic Landmark, draws tourists to hear fantastic tales—lives lived there they could not imagine. Photograph, 1995.

A huge flag was erected on the island in 2007 to celebrate American freedom and welcome visitors coming by ship. Photograph, Joe Fudge, 2007.

A passing warship reminds us of the changes Fort Wool has undergone, from riprap stone to granite casemate to concrete fire control station (top). Photograph, 2009. *David K. Hazzard.*

crane and dropped into the water below while onlookers gaped from nearby pleasure boats.

The military formally decided to end its connection with the Rip Raps in 1967. Pursuant to the terms of the original deed, the fort, the island, and the underlying bottom were turned back to the Commonwealth of Virginia. Debate has since raged over the best use for the site. In the 1970s, Virginia leased it to the City of Hampton for purposes of a historical park. After a brief interlude with visitors, Fort Wool was closed again.

In the mid-1980s, thanks to the vision of Hampton officials Mayor James L. Eason, Assistant City Manager Elizabeth A. Walker, and Parks Director Thomas H. Daniel, Fort Wool was opened to the public. The island's long stillness ended. The parade ground, then a dense jungle, came alive with a symphony of lawn mowers, weed eaters, and chain saws. A determined work crew labored several weeks removing bushes, trees, and debris. Graffiti marring the walls, including some peace signs, was removed. A retired army colonel touring the island remarked that one vandal was brazen enough to leave his name: "Led Zeppelin."

FORT WOOL

A spring morning saw Fort Wool officially reopened on May 18, 1985. United States senator John Warner's dedication speech recalled his visiting the island as a boy and his father's words: "He told me that as long as these guns are here, you'll never need to worry about your freedoms or the security of your nation." Following his speech, spectators were thrilled to observe a flyover by jet fighters from Langley Air Force Base.[177]

On Fort Wool today, antebellum, early, and mid-twentieth-century martial architecture is visible, not unlike battlements spanning the ages evident in castles and bastions in other parts of the world. The island remains virtually intact, with the exception of areas where the original line of stone has drifted. The spit formed by the stone foundation of the original wharf also remains. Sadly, only eight casemates exist, the remnants of the aesthetically beautiful Jacksonian Rip Raps. From an architectural standpoint, Fort Wool is essentially an Endicott-era work, with the greatest proportion of remaining features having originated in the early twentieth century. Battery 229 and the battery commander tower represent the modernization of the fort during the Second World War. There still needs to be breathed into these ruins something essential to the spirit of a mighty fortification, something to remind visitors of the great men who trod these stones while shaping American history. It is wonderful that thousands of new faces have come to the island of stone over the years, each experiencing it in differing ways and each taking something different away.

NOTES

Chapter 1

1. *American Beacon and Norfolk and Portsmouth Daily Advertiser*, September 2, 1829 (hereafter *American Beacon*); *Norfolk and Portsmouth Herald and General Advertiser*, July 13, 1829 (hereafter *Norfolk Herald*); *Richmond Enquirer*, July 14, 1829.
2. *Norfolk Herald*, July 13, 1829.
3. Robert V. Remini, *Andrew Jackson and the Course of American Empire, 1767–1821* (New York: Harper and Row, Publishers, 1977), 1:42.
4. Andrew Jackson to Andrew Jackson Jr., August 19, August 20, 1829, in John S. Bassett, ed., *The Correspondence of Andrew Jackson* (1969), 4:62–63.
5. Jon Meacham, *American Lion: Andrew Jackson in the White House* (New York: Random House, 2008), 67–69, 74–75; Robert V. Remini, *Andrew Jackson and the Course of American Freedom, 1822–1832* (New York: Harper and Row, Publishers, 1981), 2:161–63, 206–8, 210–12, 239–40, 306, 320–21.
6. Andrew Jackson to Andrew Jackson Donelson, August 20, 1829, in Daniel Feller and others, eds., *Papers of Andrew Jackson* (Knoxville: University of Tennessee Press, 2007), 7:387.
7. *American Beacon*, August 31, 1829.
8. Marshall Parks to Andrew Jackson, August 21–31, 1829, *Correspondence of Jackson*, 4:64–65.
9. A "roadstead" is a safe anchorage for ships. Hampton Roads is a colloquial abbreviation for "Hampton Roadstead."
10. Arthur M. Schlesinger Jr., *The Age of Jackson* (Boston: Little, Brown and Co., 1953), 369.
11. Andrew Jackson to John C. McLemore, June 27, 1831, *Correspondence of Jackson*, 4:304–6; *American Beacon*, August 11, 1833.

12. Andrew Jackson to John McLemore, June 27, 1831, and Andrew Jackson to Mary Coffee, August 15, 1833, *Correspondence of Jackson*, 4:304–5, 5:157–58.

13. Meacham, *American Lion*, 109–10.

14. Andrew Jackson to Robert J. Chester, August 8, 1833, *Correspondence of Jackson*, 5:149; *Norfolk Herald*, August 31, 1829, and July 29, 1833.

15. *Norfolk Herald*, July 8, 1831; *American Beacon*, August 7, 1835.

16. Francis P. Blair to Andrew Jackson, November 13, 1842, *Correspondence of Jackson*, 6:175–76; *New York Evening Post*, August 26, 1833.

17. Nicholas P. Trist to James Madison, July 7, 1831, Trist Papers, Virginia Historical Society; Andrew Jackson to Martin Van Buren, July 30, 1833, *Correspondence of Jackson*, 5:144–45. The *Delaware* had been the first warship repaired at the Gosport Navy Yard's new granite dry dock.

18. *American Beacon*, July 23, 1835.

19. Andrew Jackson to Robert J. Chester, August 8, 1833, *Correspondence of Jackson*, 5:149–50.

20. Pauline W. Burke, *Emily Donelson of Tennessee*, ed. Jonathan M. Atkins (Knoxville: University of Tennessee Press, 2001), 255–56.

21. James Parton, *Life of Andrew Jackson* (Boston: Houghton, Mifflin and Co., The Riverside Press, Cambridge, 1883), 3:336–37; Robert V. Remini, *Andrew Jackson and the Course of American Democracy, 1833–1845* (New York: Harper and Row, Publishers, 1984), 3:400.

Chapter 2

22. Andrew Jackson to Roger Brooke Taney, August 11, 1833, in Samuel Tyler, *Memoir of Roger Brooke Taney...* (Baltimore, MD: John Murphy & Co., 1872), 201–2.

23. *Richmond Enquirer*, September 8, 1829.

24. Andrew Jackson to John C. McLemore, June 27, 1831, *Correspondence of Jackson*, 4:304–6.

25. Schlesinger, *The Age of Jackson*, 54–55; Meacham, *American Lion*, 135–36.

26. *American Beacon*, August 11, 1833.

27. Ibid.; *Norfolk Herald*, August 16, 1833; Francis P. Blair to Martin Van Buren, November 13, 1859, in John C. Fitzpatrick, ed., *The Autobiography of Martin Van Buren* (Washington, D.C.: Government Printing Office, 1920), 2:607–8.

28. George Bancroft, "Sketch of the Life of Gen. Andrew Jackson, late president of the United States, interspersed with numerous personal anecdotes, illustrating his character and public services" (Worcester, MA: Henry J. Howland, 1845), 14.

29. Robert V. Remini, *Andrew Jackson and the Course of American Democracy*, 3:97–99.

30. Andrew Jackson to Martin Van Buren, July 30, 1833, *Correspondence of Jackson*, 5:144–45.

31. Lee quoted in Douglas Southall Freeman, *Robert E. Lee: A Biography* (New York, Charles Scribner's Sons, 1934), 1:122.

32. Andrew Jackson to Robert J. Chester, August 8, 1833, *Correspondence of Jackson*, 5:149–50.

33. Andrew Jackson to Amos Kendall, August 9, 1835, *Correspondence of Jackson*, 5:360–61.

34. *Richmond Enquirer*, July 14, 1829.

Chapter 3

35. Mary A. Bonyer to Sally W. Bibb, June 3, 1813, collections of the Hampton History Museum.

36. George G. Shackelford, "Lieutenant Lee Reports to Captain Talcott on Fort Calhoun's Construction on the Rip Raps," *Virginia Magazine of History and Biography* 60 (1952): 460.

37. Robert V. Remini, *Henry Clay: Statesman of the Union* (New York: W.W. Norton and Company, 1991), 136–37.

38. James Monroe to Andrew Jackson, December 14, 1816, *Correspondence of Jackson*, 2:269–70; John R. Weaver II, *A Legacy in Brick and Stone: American Coastal Defense Forts of the Third System, 1816–1867* (McLean, VA: Redoubt Press, 2001), 3–5.

39. Weaver, *Legacy in Brick and Stone*, 5–9, 33.

40. John C. Calhoun to Thomas M. Randolph, February 8, 1820, Edwin W. Hemphill and others, eds., *The Papers of John C. Calhoun* (Columbia: University of South Carolina Press, 1963), 4:654–55; Charles M. Wiltse, *John C. Calhoun: The Nationalist, 1782–1828* (New York: Bobbs-Merrill Co., Inc., 1944), 1:180.

41. Wiltse, *John C. Calhoun*, 1:180

Chapter 4

42. Thomas Mann Randloph to Colonel Walker K. Armistead, January 28, 1820, and John C. Calhoun to Thomas M. Randolph, February 8, 1820, and Thomas M. Randolph to John C. Calhoun, February 28, 1820, and John C. Calhoun to Thomas M. Randolph, January 26, 1821, in *Papers of Calhoun*, 4:613, 654–55, 5:503–4, 574; Richard P. Weinert Jr. and Colonel Robert Arthur, *Defender of the Chesapeake: The Story of Fort Monroe*, 3rd revised edition (Shippensburg, PA: White Mane Pub. Co., Inc., 1989), 33.

43. Charles Gratiot to Walker K. Armistead, November 30, 1819, *Papers of Calhoun*, 4:457.

44. Weinert, *Defender of the Chesapeake*, 30–31, 34; Notes in the collections of the Hampton History Museum compiled from National Archive records; *Norfolk Herald*, August 25, 1819, and July 1, 26, 1820.

45. Weinert, *Defender of the Chesapeake*, 31; Alexander Macomb to John C. Calhoun, March 2, 1825, *Papers of Calhoun*, 9:613–14; [Baltimore] *Niles' Weekly Register*, June 22, 1822.

46. http://en.wikipedia.org/wiki/Port_Deposit,_Maryland#Granite_and_bridges.

47. http://en.wikipedia.org/wiki/Scow.

48. National Archives Branch Depository, Philadelphia, PA, Corps of Engineers, Norfolk District, RG 77, "Registers of Stone Received and Costs Thereof, at Forts Monroe and Calhoun, April 1821–May 1834," 1:29–38.

49. Ibid., passim throughout volumes 1 and 2.

50. Calhoun was elected vice president first in 1824, serving under John Quincy Adams. He was reelected in 1828 to serve in Jackson's first term. In December 1832, Calhoun became the first vice president to resign, in order to accept election to the Senate.

51. Henry Clay, James F. Hopkins and Mary W.M. Hargreaves, *The Papers of Henry Clay* (Lexington: University Press of Kentucky, 1981), 6:259; *Abridgment of the Debates of Congress, from 1789 to 1856...* (New York: D. Appleton & Co., 1858), 9:416–28.

52. John C. Calhoun to Andrew Jackson, January 24, 1827, *Correspondence of Jackson*, 3:332.

53. [Baltimore] *Niles' Weekly Register*, June 22, 1822. Almost the entire issue of the *Niles'* was devoted to Fort Calhoun and the Mix contract affair.

54. Freeman, *Robert E. Lee*, 1:120.

55. Alexander Macomb to John C. Calhoun, November 24, 1821, *Papers of Calhoun*, 6:527. A "perch" is thirty cubic feet of stone.
56. *Norfolk Herald*, October 27, 1824.
57. David S. Reynolds, *Walking Giant: America in the Age of Jackson* (New York: Harper Collins Pub., 2008), 48.
58. National Archives, Records of the Office of the Chief of Engineers, RG 77, "Chief Engineer Annual Report, Fort Calhoun," November 20, 1823.

Chapter 5

59. *Niles' Weekly Register*, September 30, 1826.
60. Weaver, *Legacy in Brick and Stone*, 49–50.
61. Weinert, *Defender of the Chesapeake*, 33.
62. National Archives Branch Depository, College Park, MD, Cartographic and Architectural Branch, RG 57, "Fort Wool File," Fort Calhoun plans showing the state of the operations in 1826, 1827, 1828, and 1830.
63. National Archives, Records of the Office of the Secretary of War, RG 107, Charles Gratiot, "Report to Secretary of War, John Eaton," November 1828.
64. *American Beacon*, August 30, 1828.
65. National Archives Branch Depository, Philadelphia, PA, Corps of Engineers, Norfolk District, RG 77, "Daily Reports of Operations at Forts Monroe and Calhoun, May 1832–Dec. 1835," passim.
66. Ibid., passim.
67. National Archives Branch Depository, Philadelphia, PA, Corps of Engineers, Norfolk District, RG 77, "Daily Reports of Operations at Fort Monroe and Calhoun, Dec. 1835–Dec. 1861," 3.
68. National Archives Branch Depository, Philadelphia, PA, Corps of Engineers, Norfolk District, RG 77, "Daily Reports of Operations at Fort Monroe and Calhoun, May 1832–Dec. 1835," passim.
69. Ibid., passim.
70. *American Beacon*, August 8, 1833; John H. Schroeder, "Major Jack Downing and American Expansionism: Seba Smith's Political Satire, 1847–1856," *New England Quarterly* 50 (1977): 214–33.
71. *American Beacon*, August 11, 1833.

Chapter 6

72. Norfolk *Virginian Pilot*, November 29, 1953.
73. Charles Carter Lee to Henry Lee, July 21, 1831, http://lhome.wlu.edu/~stanleyv/LJ21jul3.1.htm.
74. Shackelford, "Lee Reports to Talcott," 471–77.
75. Robert E. Lee to Charles Gratiot, September 1, 1834, Papers of Robert E. Lee, Virginia Historical Society; Freeman, *Robert E. Lee*, 1:21.
76. Shackelford, "Lee Reports to Talcott," 471.
77. Ibid., 473.
78. National Archives Branch Depository, Philadelphia, PA, Corps of Engineers, Norfolk District, RG 77, "Daily Reports of Operations at Fort Monroe and Calhoun, May 1832–Dec. 1835," 2:165, 167.
79. Robert E. Lee to Andrew Talcott, September 12, 1833, quoted in Freeman, *Robert E. Lee*, 1:120; Shackelford, "Lee Reports to Talcott," 467.
80. National Archives Branch Depository, Philadelphia, PA, Corps of Engineers, Norfolk District, RG 77, "Letters, Reports, and Other Records Relating to Fortifications, 1810–1869," Joel Robert Poinsett to Gen. [Charles] Gratiot, July 1, 1837.
81. National Archives, Records of the Office of the Chief of Engineers, RG 77, "Chief Engineer Annual Report, Fort Calhoun," December 24, 1839.
82. Shackelford, "Lee Reports to Talcott," 484; National Archives, Records of the Office of the Chief of Engineers, RG 77, "Chief Engineer Annual Report, Fort Calhoun," November 30, 1844, and September 30, 1845.
83. *American Beacon*, October 6, 1842; *Richmond Enquirer*, October 6, 1842.
84. John Tyler to Andrew Jackson, September 20, 1842, *Correspondence of Jackson*, 6:167–68; *American Beacon*, October 6, 1842.
85. Rene E. DeRussy, Fort Monroe Record Book, April 18, 1846, Casemate Museum, Fort Monroe.
86. Benson J. Lossing, *The Pictorial Field Book of the Revolution...* (New York: Harper Bros., 1852), 2:531.

Chapter 7

87. National Archives Branch Depository, Philadelphia, PA, Corps of Engineers, Norfolk District, RG 77, "Daily Reports of Operations at Forts Monroe and Calhoun, Dec. 1835–Dec. 1861," vol. 4.

88. Phillip Shaw Paludan, *The Presidency of Abraham Lincoln* (Lawrence: University Press of Kansas), 53.

89. John Tyler to Julia G. Tyler, April 17, 1861, in Lyon G. Tyler, ed., *The Letters and Times of the Tylers* (New York: Da Capo Press, 1970), 2:641–42; Benjamin F. Butler, *Autobiography and Personal Reminiscences of Major-General Benjamin F. Butler* (Boston: A.M. Thayer and Co. Book Pub., 1892), 167.

90. National Archives, Records of the Office of the Chief of Engineers, RG 77, Entry 219, Chief Engineer to Secretary of War, "Report on "Conditions of the Forts" in Response to Resolution of House of Representatives of 31st Ultime," January 18, 1861.

91. National Archives Branch Depository, Philadelphia, PA, Corps of Engineers, Norfolk District, RG 77, "Daily Reports of Operations at Fort Calhoun, Dec. 1835–Dec. 1861," vol. 4; C. Seaforth Stewart, Captain of Engineers, to Brigadier General Joseph G. Totten, "Report," September 15, 1861.

92. Butler, *Autobiography and Personal Reminiscences*, 244.

93. Ibid., 254–55.

94. U.S. Congress, *Official Records of the Union and Confederate Navies in the War of the Rebellion* (Washington, D.C.: Government Printing Office, 1894–1922), vol. 7, series 1, 349–52. The detailed report was written after Sewell's Point and its fortifications were captured.

95. Henry Warren Howe, *Passages from the Life of Henry Warren Howe: Consisting of Diary and Letters Written During the Civil War, 1861–1865* (1899, reprint, Salem, MA: Higginson Book Co., 1970), 13–15, 20, 101; *New York Herald*, August 26, 1861.

96. Rebecca Grant Sexton, ed., *A Southern Woman of Letters: The Correspondence of Augusta Jane Evans Wilson* (Columbia: University of South Carolina Press, 2002), 33–34.

97. Benjamin F. Butler to Winfield Scott, June 20, 1861, Benjamin F. Butler, *Private and Official Correspondence of Gen. Benjamin F. Butler during the Period of the Civil War*, comp. Jessie Ames Marshall (Norwood, MA: Plimpton Press, 1917), 1:154; *National Intelligencer*, June 16, 1861; *New York Herald*, July 13, 1861.

98. F. Stansbury Haydon, *Aeronautics in the Union and Confederate Armies* (Baltimore, MD: Johns Hopkins Press, 1941), 1:93–98.

99. http://en.wikipedia.org/wiki/United_States_Army_Signal_Corps; http://en.wikipedia.org/wiki/Albert_J._Myer.

100. *New York Herald*, August 26, 1861.

101. William B. Alexander to (wife), June 6, 1861, collections of the Hampton History Museum.

102. U.S. Congress, *Official Records of Navies*, vol. 6, series 1, 310–13.

103. John V. Quarstein, *C.S.S. Virginia: Mistress of Hampton Roads* (Appomattox, VA: H.E. Howard, Inc., 2000), 77–91.

104. Ibid., 93; Philip Corell, *History of the Naval Brigade: 99ᵗʰ N.Y. Volunteers Union Coast Guard, 1861–1865* (New York: Regimental Veteran Association, 1905), 47.

105. Corell, *Naval Brigade*, 47.

106. Ibid., 132, 133; *New York Herald*, March 27, 1862.

107. U.S. Congress, *Official Records of Navies*, vol. 7, series 1, 284.

108. George Alfred Townsend, *Campaigns of a Non-Combatant and His Romaunt Abroad during the War* (1866, reprint, New York: Time-Life Books Inc., 1982), 66; *New York Herald*, February 12, 1862.

109. Weinert, *Defender of the Chesapeake*, 131; David Herbert Donald, ed., *Gone for a Soldier: The Civil War Memoirs of Private Alfred Bellard* (Boston: Little, Brown and Co., 1975), 51.

110. Townsend, *Non-Combatant*, 65–66.

Chapter 8

111. Butler, *Autobiography and Personal Reminiscences*, 42, 85, 90.

112. William H. Osborne, *The History of the Twenty-Ninth Regiment of Massachusetts Volunteer Infantry in the Late War of the Rebellion* (Boston: Albert J. Wright, Printer, 1877), 76, 83.

113. Weinert, *Defender of the Chesapeake*, 102; Corell, *Naval Brigade*, 14.

114. Corell, *Naval Brigade*, 14–15, 115.

115. National Archives Branch Depository, Philadelphia, PA, Records of the Office of the Adjutant General, RG 94, "General Order 1," November 7, 1861.

116. Butler, *Autobiography and Personal Reminiscences*, 256–58.

117. *New York Herald*, October 20, 1861.

118. Edward L. Pierce, "The Contrabands at Fortress Monroe," *Atlantic Monthly* (November 1861): 631.

119. U.S. Congress, *Official Records of Navies*, vol. 6, series 1, 311; Moss Specht to Mein Bruder, [date illegible], Collections of the Hampton History Museum.

120. Charles F. Johnson, *The Long Roll: Being a Journal of the Civil War…* (1911, reprint, Shepherdstown, WV: Carabelle Books, 1986), 37–41.

121. Committee in Behalf of the Whole to George B. McClellan, July 4, 1862, and Joseph K.F. Mansfield to John A. Dix, August 14, 1862, U.S.

Congress, *War of the Rebellion: Official Records of the Union and Confederate Armies in the War of the Rebellion* (Washington, D.C.: Government Printing Office, 1894–1922), vol. 4, series 2, 143–45, 388.

122. John A. Dix to Joseph K.F. Mansfield, August 12, 1862, *War of the Rebellion*, 377; Howe, *Life of Henry Howe*, 343.

Chapter 9

123. Edwin M. Stanton to John E. Wool, March 18, 1862, U.S. Congress, *Official Records of Armies*, vol. 11, series 1, part 3, 13.

124. James Buchanan to James B. Henry, March 29, 1862, John B. Moore, ed., *The Works of James Buchanan* (Philadelphia, PA: J.B. Lippincott Co., 1910), 11:264; William E. Beard, "The Castle of the Rip Raps," *Coast Artillery Journal* 78 (January–February 1935): 46.

125. C. Vann Woodward, ed., *Mary Chesnut's Civil War* (New Haven, CT: Yale University Press, 1981), 758.

126. Craig L. Symonds, *Lincoln and His Admirals: Abraham Lincoln, the U.S. Navy, and the Civil War* (New York: Oxford University Press, 2008), 148–55; Doris Kearns Goodwin, *Team of Rivals: The Political Genius of Abraham Lincoln* (New York: Simon and Schuster, 2005), 438–39; *New York Herald*, May 9, 1862; Corell, *Naval Brigade*, 106–7.

127. John Niven, ed., *The Salmon P. Chase Papers: Journals, 1829–1872* (Kent, OH: Kent State University Press, 1993), 1:338–39.

128. *New York Herald*, May 12, 1862.

129. U.S. Congress, *Official Records of Armies*, vol. 11, series 1, part 3, 153.

130. Niven, *Chase Journals*, 339.

131. Ibid., 338–39; Josiah Tattnall to Stephen R. Mallory, May 14, 1862, U.S. Congress, *Official Records of Navies*, vol. 7, series 1, 335–36.

132. Today the site is known as Ocean View.

133. U.S. Congress, *Official Records of Armies*, vol. 11, series 2, part 3, 429–30.

134. William Keeler to Anna Keeler May 10, 1862, Robert W. Daly, ed., *Aboard the USS Monitor: 1862, the Letters of Acting Paymaster William Frederick Keeler, U.S. Navy To His Wife, Anna*, Naval Letters Series (Annapolis, MD: United States Naval Institute, 1964), 1:117.

135. U.S. Congress, *Official Records of Armies*, vol. 11, series 1, part 1, 635.

136. Symonds, *Lincoln and His Admirals*, 155–56; James M. McPherson, "Commander in Chief," *Smithsonian* 39 (January 2009): 45.

137. Townsend, *Non-Combatant*, 63–64.

138. Seaforth Stewart to Secretary of War, *Annual Report of the Progress Made in the Construction of Fort Wool, Hampton Roads, Va. for the year ending June 30th 1864*, collections of the Hampton History Museum.

139. Michael Burlingame and John R. Turner Ettlinger, eds., *Inside Lincoln's White House: The Complete Civil War Diary of John Hay* (Carbondale: Southern Illinois University Press, 1997), 190.

Chapter 10

140. National Archives Branch Depository, Philadelphia, PA, Corps of Engineers, Norfolk District, RG 77, "Letters Sent Forts Monroe and Wool, 1872–1879," William P. Craighill to Andrew A. Humphreys, March 21, 1873.

141. John J. Craven, *Prison Life of Jefferson Davis…* (1866, reprint, Biloxi, MS: Souvenir Shop, Jefferson Davis Shrine, 1960), 204–7.

142. National Archives Branch Depository, Philadelphia, PA, Corps of Engineers, Norfolk District, RG 77, "Letters Sent Forts Monroe and Wool, 1872–1879," William P. Craighill to Andrew A. Humphreys, July 26, 1872, and June 30, 1874.

143. Weinert, *Defender of the Chesapeake*, 168–69.

144. Poe was stationed at Fort Monroe in 1828–29, and while there is no documentation, he probably visited the Rip Raps.

Chapter 11

145. Weinert, *Defender of the Chesapeake*, 190–91.

146. Ibid., 208; Terrance McGovern and Bolling Smith, *American Coastal Defenses 1885–1950* (New York: Osprey Publishing Limited, 2006), 31–33, 37.

147. U.S. Engineer Department, "Proposals for Work," January 16, 1904, and February 8, 1904.

148. Weinert, *Defender of the Chesapeake*, 218 n. 35.

149. U.S. War Department, *Harbor Defenses Fort Wool & Related* (CD-Rom), Battery Jacob Hindman, July 1, 1919, Battery Henry Lee, July 1, 1919, Battery Claiborne, July 1, 1919, Battery Dyer, December 1, 1928, Battery Horatio Gates, December 18, 1928 (Bel Air, MD: The Coast Defense Study Group Press, 2008).

150. William H. Lee, *Laird and Lee's Guide to Historic Virginia, and the Jamestown Centennial* (1907, reprint, San Antonio, TX: Vision Forum, Inc., 2007), 45–46.
151. U.S. War Department, *Fort Wool* (CD-Rom), Barracks, November 15, 1910.
152. Ibid., Water Tank, 1910.
153. Ibid., Supplementary Station, April 2, 1928.
154. Mary W. Gray, *Gloucester County Virginia* (Richmond, VA: Cottrell and Cooke, Inc., 1936), 143.
155. National Archives Branch Depository, Philadelphia, PA, Chesapeake Bay File, RG 77, entry 220, "Plan of Fort Wool," revisions of April 1, 1921.
156. U.S. War Department, *Fort Wool* (CD-Rom), Coincidence Range Finder Station, April 2, 1928.
157. Personal communication from Elizabeth Newton, summer 1993; Norfolk *Virginian Pilot*, October 27, 1949; Horace L. Gifford to J. Michael Cobb, May 31, 1991, collections of the Hampton History Museum.

Chapter 12

158. Weinert, *Defender of the Chesapeake*, 262–64.
159. Ibid., 274, 280–81; Paul S. Morando and David J. Johnson, *Fort Monroe* (Charleston, SC: Arcadia Publishing, 2008), 79.
160. Alec Guinness, *Blessings in Disguise* (New York: Alfred A. Knopf, 1985), 119 (New Year's Day, 1944).
161. Newport News *Daily Press*, December 9, 1941.
162. M.G. Stroud to Joseph Frankowski, February [n.d.], 1988, collections of the Hampton History Museum.
163. Horace L. Gifford to J. Michael Cobb, May 31, 1991, collections of the Hampton History Museum; Christmas Menu [for troops on Fort Wool, December 25,] 1941, collections of the Hampton History Museum.
164. Norfolk *Ledger Star*, October 27, 1949; Richmond *Times-Dispatch*, November 6, 1949.
165. Horace L. Gifford to J. Michael Cobb, May 31, 1991, collections of the Hampton History Museum.
166. U.S. War Department, *Fort Wool* (CD-Rom), B.C. and C.R.F. Station, January 31, 1943.
167. Thomas Fazenbacker, telephone conversation with J. Michael Cobb, October 24, 2008.

168. U.S. War Department, *Fort Wool* (CD-Rom), SCR-296, October 22, 1943.

169. U.S. War Department, *Fort Wool* (CD-Rom), B.C. and C.R.F. Station, October 22, 1943.

170. Norfolk *Virginian Pilot*, October 27, 1949.

171. Thomas Fazenbacker, telephone conversation with J. Michael Cobb, October 24, 2008.

172. Horace L. Gifford, personal communication to J. Michael Cobb, June 2002.

Chapter 13

173. "Life on the Rock," undated U.S. Army publication, circa 1946, before the base was closed.

174. Ray C. Alexander to J. Michael Cobb, January 13, 1986, collections of the Hampton History Museum.

175. Newport News *Daily Press*, June 1, 1952.

176. Norfolk *Virginian Pilot*, November 29, 1953.

177. *Remarks of Senator John Warner Opening of Fort Wool…*, May 18, 1985, collections of the Hampton History Museum.

BIBLIOGRAPHY

Primary Sources

Manuscripts and Manuscript Collections

Charles Carter Lee to Henry Lee, July 21, 1831. http://lhome.wlu.edu/~stanleyv/LJ21jul3.1.htm.

Collections. Hampton History Museum, Hampton, Virginia.

Fort Monroe Record Book. Casemate Museum, Fort Monroe, Virginia.

National Archives Branch Depository, College Park, Maryland. Cartographic and Architectural Branch. Fort Wool File. RG 57.

National Archives Branch Depository, Philadelphia, Pennsylvania. Chesapeake Bay File. RG 77.

———. Records of the Corps of Engineers, Norfolk District. RG 77.

———. Records of the Office of Adjutant General. RG 94.

National Archives. Records of the Office of the Chief of Engineers. RG 77.

———. Records of the Office of the Secretary of War. RG 107.

Robert E. Lee Papers. Virginia Historical Society, Richmond, Virginia.

Trist Papers. Virginia Historical Society, Richmond, Virginia.

Published Sources

Abridgment of the Debates of Congress, from 1789 to 1856... New York: D. Appleton & Company, 1858.

Bancroft, George. *Sketch of the Life of Gen. Andrew Jackson, Late President of the United States...* Worcester, MA: Henry J. Howland, 1845.

Bassett, John Spencer, ed. *The Correspondence of Andrew Jackson.* 6 vols. 1926–1933. Reprint, New York: Kraus Reprint Company, 1969.

Burlingame, Michael, and John R. Turner Ettlinger, eds. *Inside Lincoln's White House: The Complete Civil War Diary of John Hay.* Carbondale: Southern Illinois Press, 1977.

Butler, Benjamin F. *Autobiography and Personal Reminiscences of Major-General Benjamin F. Butler.* Boston: A.M. Thayer and Co., Book Pub., 1892.

Clay, Henry, James F. Hopkins, and Mary W. Hargreaves. *The Papers of Henry Clay.* 10 vols. Lexington: University Press of Kentucky, 1959–1991.

Craven, John J. *Prison Life of Jefferson Davis...* 1866. Reprint, Biloxi, MS: Souvenir Shop, Jefferson Davis Shrine, 1960.

Daly, Robert W., ed. *Aboard the USS Monitor: 1862, The Letter of Acting Paymaster William Frederick Keeler, U.S. Navy, to His Wife, Anna.* Annapolis, MD: United States Naval Institute, 1964.

Donald, David Herbert, ed. *Gone for a Soldier: The Civil War Memoirs of Private Alfred Bellard.* Boston: Little, Brown and Co., 1975.

Feller, Daniel, Harold D. Moser, Laura-Eve Moss, and Thomas Coens, eds. *Papers of Andrew Jackson.* Vol. 7. Knoxville: University of Tennessee Press, 2007.

Fitzpatrick, John C., ed. *The Autobiography of Martin Van Buren.* 2 vols. Washington, D.C.: Government Printing Office, 1920.

Hemphill, Edwin W., ed. *The Papers of John C. Calhoun.* Vols. 5 and 6. Columbia: University of South Carolina Press, 1963.

Howe, Henry Warren. *Passages from the Life of Henry Warren Howe: Consisting of Diary and Letters Written During the Civil War, 1861–1865.* 1899. Reprint, Salem, MA: Higginson Book Company, 1970.

Johnson, Charles F. *The Long Roll: Being a Journal of the Civil War.* 1911. Reprint, Shepherdstown, WV: Carabelle Books, 1986.

Lossing, Benson J. *The Pictorial Field Book of the Revolution.* 2 vols. New York: Harper Bros., 1852.

Marshall, Jessie Ames, comp. *Private and Official Correspondence of Gen. Benjamin F. Butler During the Period of the Civil War.* 6 vols. Norwood, MA: Plimpton Press, 1917.

Moore, John Bassett, ed. *The Works of James Buchanan: Comprising His Speeches, State Papers, and Private Correspondence.* 11 vols. Philadelphia, PA: J.B. Lippincott Company, 1910.

Niven, John, ed. *The Salmon P. Chase Papers: Journals, 1829–1872.* Vol. 1. Kent, OH: Kent State University Press, 1993.

Sexton, Rebecca Grant, ed. *A Southern Woman of Letters: The Correspondence of Augusta Jane Evans Wilson.* Columbia: University of South Carolina Press, 2002.

Townsend, George Alfred. *Campaigns of a Non-Combatant, and His Romaunt Abroad During the War.* Reprint, New York: Time-Life Books, 1982.

Tyler, Lyon G., ed. *The Letters and Times of the Tylers.* New York: Da Capo Press, 1970.

Tyler, Samuel, ed. *Memoir of Roger Brooke Taney.* Baltimore, MD: John Murphy and Company, 1872.

U.S. Congress. *Official Records of the Union and Confederate Navies in the War of the Rebellion.* 30 vols. Washington, D.C.: Government Printing Office, 1894–1922.

————. *War of the Rebellion: Official Records of the Union and Confederate Armies in the War of the Rebellion.* 128 vols. Washington, D.C.: Government Printing Office, 1894–1922.

U.S. War Department. *Harbor Defenses Fort Wool & Related* (CD-Rom). Bel Air, MD: The Coast Defense Study Group Press, 2008.

Woodward, C. Vann, ed. *Mary Chesnut's Civil War.* New Haven, CT: Yale University Press, 1981.

Periodicals

American Beacon and Norfolk and Portsmouth Daily Advertiser
Baltimore Niles' Weekly Register
Frank Leslie's Illustrated Newspaper
Harper's Weekly: Journal of Civilization
National Intelligencer
Newport News *Daily Press*
New York Herald
Norfolk and Portsmouth Herald and General Advertiser
Norfolk Ledger-Dispatch
Norfolk *Virginian Pilot*
Richmond Enquirer
Richmond Times-Dispatch
Washington Globe

Secondary Sources

Books

Barnes, Emma L. *Rip Raps.* 1892.

Burke, Pauline Wilcox. *Emily Donelson of Tennessee.* Edited by Jonathan M. Atkins. Knoxville: University of Tennessee Press, 2001.

Coffman, Edward M. *The Old Army: A Portrait of the American Army in Peacetime 1784–1898.* New York: Oxford University Press, 1986.

Corell, Philip. *History of the Naval Brigade: 99ᵗʰ N.Y. Volunteers Union Coast Guard.* New York: Regimental Veteran Association, 1905.

Emmerson, John C., Jr., ed. *The Steamboat Comes to Norfolk Harbour, and the Log of the First Ten Years; 1815–1825.* Portsmouth, VA: John C. Emmerson Jr., 1947.

Freehling, William W. *Prelude to Civil War: The Nullification Controversy in South Carolina, 1816–1836.* New York: Oxford University Press, 1965.

Freeman, Douglas Southall. *Robert E. Lee: A Biography.* 4 vols. New York: Charles Scribner's Sons, 1934.

Goodwin, Doris Kearns. *Team of Rivals: The Political Genius of Abraham Lincoln.* New York: Simon & Schuster, 2005.

Gray, Mary W. *Gloucester County Virginia.* Richmond, VA: Cottrell and Cooke, Inc., 1936.

Guinness, Alec. *Blessings in Disguise.* New York: Alfred A. Knopf, 1986.

Haydon, F. Stansbury. *Aeronautics in the Union and Confederate Armies.* Vol. 1. Baltimore, MD: Johns Hopkins University Press, 1941.

Holt, Michael F. *The Rise and Fall of the American Whig Party: Jacksonian Politics and the Onset of the Civil War.* New York: Oxford University Press, 1999.

Lee, William H. *Laird and Lee's Guide to Historic Virginia and the Jamestown Centennial.* 1907. Reprint, San Antonio, TX: Vision Forum, 2007.

Lews, Emanuel Raymond. *Seacoast Fortifications of the United States: An Introductory History.* Seventh edition. Annapolis, MD: Naval Institute Press, 1979.

McGovern, Terrance, and Bolling Smith. *American Coastal Defenses 1885–1950.* New York: Osprey Publishing Limited, 2006.

Meacham, Jon. *American Lion: Andrew Jackson in the White House.* New York: Random House, 2008.

Morando, Paul S., and David J. Johnson. *Fort Monroe*. Charleston, SC: Arcadia Publishing, 2008.

Osborne, William H. *The History of the Twenty-Ninth Regiment of Massachusetts Volunteer Infantry; In the Late War of the Rebellion*. Boston: Albert J. Wright, Printer, 1877.

Paludan, Phillip Shaw. *The Presidency of Abraham Lincoln*. Lawrence: University Press of Kansas, 1994.

Parton, James. *Life of Andrew Jackson*. 3 vols. Boston: Houghton Mifflin Company, The Riverside Press, Cambridge, 1883.

Quarstein, John V. *C.S.S. Virginia: Mistress of Hampton Roads*. Appomattox, VA: H.E. Howard, Inc., 2000.

Remini, Robert V. *Andrew Jackson and the Course of American Democracy, 1833–1845*. Vol. 3. New York: Harper and Row, Publishers, 1984.

———. *Andrew Jackson and the Course of American Empire, 1767–1821*. Vol. 1. New York: Harper and Row, Publishers, 1977.

———. *Andrew Jackson and the Course of American Freedom, 1822–1832*. Vol. 2. New York: Harper and Row, Publishers, 1981.

———. *Henry Clay: Statesman for the Union*. New York: W.W. Norton and Company, 1991.

Reynolds, David S. *Walking Giant: America in the Age of Jackson*. New York: Harper Collins Publishers, 2008.

Schlesinger, Arthur M., Jr. *The Age of Jackson*. Boston: Little, Brown and Company, 1953.

Symonds, Craig L. *Lincoln and His Admirals: Abraham Lincoln, the U.S. Navy, and the Civil War*. New York: Oxford University Press, 2008.

Weaver, John, II. *A Legacy in Brick and Stone: American Coastal Defense Forts of the Third System, 1816–1867*. McLean, VA: Redoubt Press, 2001.

Weinert, Richard P., Jr., and Colonel Robert Arthur. *Defender of the Chesapeake: The Story of Fort Monroe.* Third revised edition. Shippensburg, PA: White Mane Publishing Company, 1989.

Wiltse, Charles M. *John C. Calhoun.* Vol. 1. *Nationalist, 1782–1828.* Indianapolis, IN: Bobbs-Merrill Company, Inc., 1944.

———. *John C. Calhoun.* Vol. 2. *Nullifier, 1829–1839.* Indianapolis, IN: Bobbs-Merrill Company, Inc., 1949.

Articles

"Albert J. Myer." Wikipedia, the free encyclopedia. http://en.wikipedia.org/wiki/Albert_J._Myer.

Beard, William E. "The Castle of Rip Raps." *Coast Artillery Journal* 78 (January–February 1935): 44–46.

McPherson, James M. "Commander in Chief." *Smithsonian* 39, no. 10 (January 2009): 38–45.

Pierce, Edward L. "The Contrabands at Fortress Monroe." *Atlantic Monthly* (November 1861): 626–40.

"Port Deposit, Maryland." Wikipedia, the free encyclopedia. http://en.wikipedia.org/wiki/Port_Deposit,_Maryland#Granite_and_bridges.

Schroeder, John H. "Major Jack Downing and American Expansionism: Seba Smith's Political Satire, 1847–1856." *New England Quarterly* 50 (1977): 214–33.

"Scow." Wikipedia, the free encyclopedia. http://en.wikipedia.org/wiki/Scow.

Shackelford, George G. "Lieutenant Lee Reports to Captain Talcott on Fort Calhoun's Construction on the Rip Raps." *Virginia Magazine of History and Biography* 60 (1952): 471–77.

"Signal Corps (United States Army)." Wikipedia, the free encyclopedia. http://en.wikipedia.org/wiki/United_States_Army_Signal_Corps.

Visit us at
www.historypress.net